THE CYBERSECURITY BIBLE

[5 in 1] The All-In-One Guide to Detect, Prevent, and Manage Cyber Threats. Includes Hands-On Exercises to Become an Expert and Lead Your (First) Security Team

Rick C. Worley

© Copyright Rick C. Worley 2023 - All rights reserved.

The content contained within this book may not be reproduced, duplicated, or transmitted without direct written permission from the author or the publisher.

Under no circumstances will any blame or legal responsibility be held against the publisher, or author, for any damages, reparation, or monetary loss due to the information contained within this book. Either directly or indirectly.

Legal Notice:

This book is copyright protected. This book is only for personal use. You cannot amend, distribute, sell, use, quote, or paraphrase any part, or the content within this book, without the consent of the author or publisher.

Disclaimer Notice:

Please note the information contained within this document is for educational and entertainment purposes only. All effort has been executed to present accurate, up-to-date, and reliable, complete information. No warranties of any kind are declared or implied. Readers acknowledge that the author is not engaging in the rendering of legal, financial, medical, or professional advice. The content within this book has been derived from various sources. Please consult a licensed professional before attempting any techniques outlined in this book.

By reading this document, the reader agrees that under no circumstances is the author responsible for any losses, direct or indirect, which are incurred as a result of the use of the information contained within this document, including, but not limited to, — errors, omissions, or inaccuracies.

The book cover has been designed using resources from Freepik.com

TABLE OF CONTENTS

INTRODUCTION	**18**
BOOK 1: FUNDAMENTALS OF CYBERSECURITY	**21**
CHAPTER 1: CYBERSECURITY BASICS	22
Defining Cybersecurity	**22**
What is Cybersecurity?	23
Some Key Responsibilities of Cybersecurity	23
Scope and Domains of Cybersecurity	24
The CIA Triad: Confidentiality, Integrity, and Availability	**25**
Confidentiality	25
Integrity	26
Availability	27
Evolution of the CIA Triad	28
Implementing the CIA Triad	29
Common Cyber Threats	**30**
Malware	30
Ransomware	30
Phishing and Social Engineering	30
Identity Theft	31
Hacking	31
Distributed Denial of Service (DDoS) Attacks	31
Insider Threats	32
Supply Chain Attacks	32
Cloud Security Breaches	32
IoT/Operational Technology Attacks	33
Wireless Network Attacks	33
Encryption Attacks	33
CHAPTER 2: RISK ASSESSMENT AND MANAGEMENT	34
Identifying Vulnerabilities	**34**
Mapping Assets	34
Third-Party Relationships	35
Monitoring Asset Inventory	36
Mapping Data Flows	36
Identifying Software Vulnerabilities	37

    Identifying Configuration Vulnerabilities — 37
    Identifying People Vulnerabilities — 38
    Identifying Process Vulnerabilities — 38
Assessing Risk — **38**
    Risk Identification — 38
    Risk Analysis — 39
    Risk Evaluation — 39
    Control Assessment — 39
    Treatment Options — 39
    Policy and Process Review — 39
    Risk Monitoring — 40
    Communication and Training — 40
Risk Mitigation Strategies — **40**
    Assessing Current State — 40
    Technical Controls — 40
    Procedural Controls — 41
    Testing Effectiveness — 41
    Technology Environments — 41
    Residual Risk Acceptance — 41
    Third-Party Dependencies — 42
    Communication and Training — 42
    Monitoring and Improvement — 42
    Third-Party Risk Management — 42
    Departmental Coordination — 42
    Crisis Communications — 43
    Regulatory Compliance — 43

CHAPTER 3: SECURITY POLICIES AND PROCEDURES — 44
Creating a Security Policy — **44**
    Stakeholder Engagement — 44
    Research Regulatory Requirements — 45
    Assess Existing Controls — 45
    Draft Content — 45
    Policy Sections — 45
    Review Cycles — 45
    Approval Workflow — 46
    Publish and Socialize — 46
    Monitoring and Enforcement — 46
    Evaluate Effectiveness — 46
    Strategic Alignment — 46
Enforcing Security Procedures — **47**
    Auditing Compliance — 47
    Training Alignment — 47
    Monitoring Activities — 47

    Vulnerability Remediation   47
    Account Management   48

Incident Response Coordination   **48**
    Change Management   48
    Digital Evidence Management   48
    Performance Management   48
    Departmental Ownership   49
    Escalation Management   49
    Vendor Risk Management   49
    User Reporting   49
    Metrics and Reporting   49
    Incident Response Plans   50
    Roles and Responsibilities   50
    Initial Response   50
    Data Collection and Preservation   50
    Incident Classification   50
    Investigation Procedures   50
    Communications Plans   51
    Vulnerability Assessments   51
    Restoration and Recovery   51
    Exercises and Improvements   51
    Reporting and Notification   51
    Triage and Prioritization   52
    Forensic Investigations   52
    Incident Documentation   52
    CSIRT Coordination   52
    After Action Reviews   52
    Metrics and Reporting   52

CHAPTER 4: LEGAL AND ETHICAL CONSIDERATIONS   53

Data Privacy Regulations   **53**
    Compliance Landscape   53
    Personal Data Definitions   54
    Consent and Purpose Limitation   54
    Data Subject Rights   54
    Data Inventory and Mapping   54
    Data Protection by Design and Default   55
    Data Minimization and Retention   55
    Data Transfers and Accountability   55
    Breach Notification and Response   55

Ethical Hacking and Penetration Testing   **56**
    Risk Assessments   56
    Planning and Approvals   56
    Methodology Definition   56

Tester Qualifications	57
Environment Isolation	57
Discovery and Exploitation	57
Reporting and Remediation	**57**
Exercises and Improvements	57
Reporting Security Incidents	58
Roles and Responsibilities	58
Detection Techniques	58
Initial Response	58
Classification and Assessment	58
Communications Protocols	59
Investigation Techniques	59
Remediation Strategies	59
Post-Incident Review	59

BOOK 2: NETWORK SECURITY — 60

CHAPTER 5: NETWORK SECURITY FUNDAMENTALS — 61

Network Topologies — **61**

Star Topology	61
Ring Topology	62
Bus Topology	62
Mesh Topology	62
Tree Topology	63
Hybrid Topologies	63
Wireless Topologies	63
Infrastructure Mode	63
Ad-Hoc Mode	64
Hybrid Wireless-Wired	64

Encryption and VPNs — **64**

Encryption	64
Virtual Private Networks	65

Firewall and Intrusion Detection Systems — **68**

Firewalls	68
Intrusion Detection Systems	70

CHAPTER 6: SECURE NETWORK DESIGN — 72

Subnetting and IP Addressing — **72**

Internet Protocol Version 4	72
Classful Networking	73
Subnetting	73
Subnet Masks	73
Variable Length Subnet Masks	73
Address Depletion Mitigations	74

Subnet Design Considerations … 74
Addressing IoT and Cloud … 74
Addressing Virtualization … 75
Addressing Security … 75

DMZs and Segmentation … **75**
Network Segmentation … 75
Demilitarized Zones … 76
Segmentation Design … 76
Segmentation Techniques … 77
Risks of Poor Segmentation … 77
Software-Defined Segmentation … 77
Hybrid Cloud Segmentation … 77

Securing Wireless Networks … **78**
Wireless Networking Growth and Risks … 78
Wireless Encryption … 78
SSID Broadcasting … 78
MAC Address Filtering … 79
Rogue AP Detection … 79
Guest Network Isolation … 79
Network Perimeter Security … 79
Wireless Access Controls … 80
Signal Hardening … 80

CHAPTER 7: NETWORK MONITORING AND THREAT DETECTION … 81

Network Traffic Analysis … **81**
Network Traffic and Infrastructure Visibility … 81
Network TAPs and Spanning … 82
Capturing and Storage … 82
Deep Packet Inspection … 82
Traffic Decryption … 82
Analytics Techniques … 83
Traffic Analysis Tools … 83
Compliance and Privacy … 83

Detecting Anomalies … **84**
Establishing Baselines … 84
Behavioral Analysis … 84
External Context … 84
Investigation and Tuning … 85
Anomaly Types … 85
Detection Challenges … 85
Regulatory Considerations … 85

Responding to Network Incidents … **86**
Incident Response Planning … 86
Incident Detection … 86

Initial Response	86
On-Site Response	86
Tactical Analysis	87
Short Term Remediation	87
Long Term Remediation	87
Post Incident Activities	87
Sharing Economy	88

CHAPTER 8: ADVANCED NETWORK SECURITY	**89**
Zero Trust Architecture	**89**
Trust Paradigm Evolution	89
Zero Trust Principles	90
Microsegmentation	90
Access Controls	90
Privacy and Usability	90
Tools and Technologies	91
Adoption Challenges	91
Advanced Firewall Configurations	**92**
Firewall Fundamentals	92
Packet Filtering	92
Threat Intelligence	92
Web Application Firewalls	93
Microsegmentation	93
Orchestration	93
Artificial Intelligence	93
Secure Cloud Networking	**94**
Cloud Networking Benefits	94
Network Segmentation	94
Network Access	94
Cloud Network Security	95
Hybrid Integration	95
Visibility and Analytics	96

BOOK 3: WEB AND APPLICATION SECURITY	**97**
CHAPTER 9: WEB SECURITY PRINCIPLES	**98**
OWASP Top Ten	**98**
OWASP Top Ten	98
History and Methodology	99
Impact of the Top Ten	99
Categories and Risks	99
Mitigation Strategies	100
Tools and Technologies	100
Prioritizing Remediation	101

Organizational Alignment — 101

Secure Coding Practices — 102
Secure Development Lifecycle — 102
Planning and Requirements — 102
Secure Coding Practices — 102
Configuration Management — 103
Code Reviews — 103
Testing — 103
Training and Tools — 103
Deployment and Operations — 104

Web Application Firewalls — 104
Inspecting HTTP Requests and Responses — 104
Rule Configuration and Management — 105
Deployments and Placements — 105
Detection and Prevention Techniques — 105
Administration and Management — 106

CHAPTER 10: SECURING DATABASES AND DATA — 107

Database Security — 107
Introduction to Database Security — 107
Physical and Environmental Security — 108
Network Segregation and Encryption — 108
Identity and Access Management — 108
Configuration Hardening — 108
Monitoring and Logging — 109
Vulnerability Management — 109
API and Web Application Security — 109
Identity and Access Management Considerations — 110
Audit and Compliance Assurance — 110
Third-Party Risk Management — 110

Data Encryption — 111
Importance of Data Encryption — 111
Encryption Algorithms — 111
Key Management — 112
Implementation Considerations — 112

Data Backup and Recovery — 112
Why Backup and Recovery Matters — 112
Defining Recovery Objectives — 113
Backup Methodologies — 113
On-premise Backup — 113
Cloud Backup — 114
Backup Monitoring — 114
Recovery Fundamentals — 114

CHAPTER 11: SECURING MOBILE AND IOT DEVICES — 115

Mobile Device Management — 115
- Enrollment and Authentication — 116
- Inventory & Compliance — 116
- Application Management — 116
- Security & Encryption — 116
- Help Desk Support — 117
- Analytics & Reporting — 117

IoT Security Challenges — 117
- The Emergence of IoT — 117
- Device Heterogeneity — 117
- Resource Limitations — 118
- Insecure Defaults — 118
- Fragmented Development — 118
- Operational Challenges — 118

Best Practices for Mobile and IoT Security — 119
- Access Controls — 119
- Configuration Security — 119
- Application Controls — 120
- Anomaly Detection — 120
- Incident Response — 120

CHAPTER 12: CLOUD SECURITY — 121

Cloud Service Models — 121
- Cloud Computing — 121
- Infrastructure as a Service — 122
- Platform as a Service — 122
- Software as a Service — 122
- Choosing Models — 122
- Pricing Structures — 123

Shared Responsibility Model — 123
- Data in the Cloud — 123
- Shared Infrastructure Security — 124
- Platform and Applications — 124
- Network and Perimeter Security — 124
- Incident Response — 124

Cloud Security Best Practices — 125
- Access Management — 125
- Network Security — 125
- Infrastructure Protection — 125
- Application Security — 126
- Identity Federation — 126
- Data Protection — 126
- Configuration Management — 126

Vulnerability Management	127
Logging and Monitoring	127
Supply Chain Security	127
Governance	127
Incident Response	127

BOOK 4: ENDPOINT SECURITY AND USER AWARENESS — 128

CHAPTER 13: ENDPOINT SECURITY — 129

Antivirus and Anti-Malware — **129**

What are Antivirus and Anti-Malware?	129
How Antivirus Works	130
Types of Antivirus Protection	130
Key Features to Consider	131
Deployment	131
Configuration	132
Signature Updates	132
Heuristics and Behavioral Analysis	132
Reporting and Analytics	132
Training and Support	133
Integration and Maintenance	133

Endpoint Security Solutions — **133**

Endpoint Detection and Response	133
Next-generation Antivirus	134
Application Control	134
Device Control and Encryption	134
Endpoint Security Suites	135

BYOD Policies — **135**

Policy Purpose and Objectives	135
Device Eligibility and Registration	135
Acceptable Use Standards	136
Security Requirements	136
Risk Acknowledgment	136
Access Management	136
Data Handling Standards	136
Compliance Measures	137
Support and Enforcement	137
BYOD Program Launch	137
Technical Configuration	137
Data Loss Prevention	137
Compliance Verification	138
Governance Oversight	138
Training and Culture	138
Continuous Improvement	138

CHAPTER 14: USER TRAINING AND AWARENESS — 139
Social Engineering Awareness — **139**
- Understanding Social Engineering — 139
- Impact of Social Engineering — 140
- Training Goals and Focus Areas — 140
- Designing Effective Training — 140
- Preparing the Learning Environment — 141
- Reinforcement and Continual Improvement — 141
- Metrics and Tracking — 141
- Practical Considerations — 141

Phishing Detection and Prevention — **142**
- Technical Detection — 142
- Blocklisting and Whitelisting — 142
- DMARC/DKIM Email Authentication — 143
- URL Shortener Monitoring — 143
- Targeted Education and Training — 143
- Policy and Process — 143
- Metrics and Oversight — 144

User Behavior Analytics — **144**
- Modeling Normal Behavior — 144
- Use Cases for Detection — 144
- Investigation and Response — 145
- Monitoring Privileged Accounts — 145
- Implementation Roadmap — 145
- Addressing Privacy Concerns — 145
- Preparing the Environment — 146
- Educating Stakeholders — 146
- Analyst Training — 146
- Metrics and Optimization — 146
- Third-Party UBA — 147

CHAPTER 15: INSIDER THREAT DETECTION AND MITIGATION — 148
Insider Threat Indicators — **148**
- Technical Activity Monitoring — 148
- Policies and User Agreements — 149
- Privileged User Oversight — 149
- Behavioral Indicators — 149
- Investigation Techniques — 149
- Resolution and Support — 149
- Program Socialization — 150
- Metrics and Tracking — 150
- Continual Improvement — 150
- Stakeholders and Communication — 150

Monitoring Employee Activities — 151
- Establishing Objectives — 151
- Selecting Monitoring Tools — 151
- Controlling Tool Configurations — 151
- Updating Access Policies — 151
- Incident Response — 152
- Privacy by Design — 152
- Socializing the Program — 152
- Metrics and Program Improvement — 152
- Governance and Oversight — 152
- Third-Party Considerations — 153

Responding to Insider Threats — 153
- Planning the Response — 153
- Initiating Response — 153
- Containment Measures — 154
- Conducting Investigations — 154
- Resolving Confirmed Issues — 154
- Crisis Communications — 155
- After Action Review — 155
- Individual Support Considerations — 155
- Metrics and Continuous Improvement — 155
- Third-Party Extension — 156
- International Coordination — 156
- Prevention integration — 156

CHAPTER 16: SECURITY COMPLIANCE AND AUDITING — 157

Regulatory Compliance — 157
- Assessing Regulatory Landscape — 157
- Documentation and Controls — 158
- Ongoing Auditing and Testing — 158
- Training and Awareness — 158
- Incident Response — 158
- Data Governance — 158
- Metrics and Oversight — 159
- Third-Party Management — 159
- Individual Rights Management — 159
- Privacy by Design — 159
- Compliance as a Competitive Differentiator — 160

Security Auditing — 160
- Planning the Audit — 160
- Pre-engagement Activity — 160
- On-site Fieldwork — 160
- Control Evaluation and Reporting — 161
- Follow-up Engagement — 161

Quality Assurance	161
Selecting Audit Types	161
Personnel Audits	161
External Auditing Considerations	162
Metrics and Maturity Assessment	162
Regulatory Evaluation Coordination	162

Compliance Reporting and Documentation — **162**

Defining Report Types	163
Designing Templates	163
Collecting Source Data	163
Quality Assurance	163
Distributing Reports	163
Analytics and Visualization	164
Archiving and Retention	164
Operationalizing Documentation	164
Maturity Assessments	164
Regulatory Filings	164
International Considerations	165
Succession Planning	165

BOOK 5: LEADERSHIP AND HANDS-ON EXERCISES — 166

CHAPTER 17: LEADING YOUR SECURITY TEAM — 167

Building a Security Team — **167**

Establishing Skill Requirements	167
Recruiting Team Members	168
Developing Through Training	168
Fostering the Right Culture	168
Performance Management	169
Keeping The Team Secure	169
Managing the Team	169

Leadership in Cybersecurity — **170**

Establishing Vision and Goals	171
Gaining Internal Influence	171
Compliance and Governance	171
Leading Through Adversity	171
Building Talent and Succession	172
Developing Strategic Partnerships	172
Managing Projects and Budgets	172

Managing Security Projects — **173**

Defining Project Scope	174
Developing Comprehensive Plans	174

CHAPTER 18: INCIDENT RESPONSE AND RECOVERY — 175

Incident Handling Procedures — **175**
- Establishing Clear Roles and Responsibilities — 175
- Training and Exercising the Plan — 176
- Detection and Initial Response — 176
- Investigation and Analysis — 176
- Remediation, Recovery, and Communication — 176
- Policy, Regulation, and Lessons Learned — 176
- Exercising Continuous Improvement — 177
- Detecting and Responding to Incidents — 177

Forensics and Investigation — **178**
- Planning and Preparation — 178
- Evidence Identification, Preservation, and Documentation — 178
- Live Response and Memory Forensics — 179
- Non-Volatile Data Acquisition and Examination — 179
- Evidence Processing and Investigation — 179
- Reporting and Continuous Improvement — 179

Business Continuity and Disaster Recovery — **180**
- Impact Assessments and Prioritization — 180
- Recovery Strategies — 180
- Emergency Response Procedures — 180
- Activation and Recovery Operations — 181
- Infrastructure and Environmental Monitoring — 181
- Critical Data Protection — 182
- Team Preparedness — 182
- Continuous Improvement — 182

CHAPTER 19: SECURITY CULTURE AND AWARENESS PROGRAMS — 183

Creating a Security Culture — **183**
- Communications and Training — 184
- Data Stewardship and Handling — 184
- User-Focused Security — 184
- Internal Reporting — 185

Security Awareness Training Programs — **185**
- Needs Assessment — 185
- Curriculum Design — 186
- Awareness Exercises — 186
- Communications and Resources — 187
- Continuous Improvement — 187

Measuring the Effectiveness of Awareness Initiatives — **187**
- Defining Objectives — 188
- Choosing Metrics — 188
- Data Collection — 188
- Analyzing Results — 189
- Communicating Insights — 189

Review and Improvement	189
Benchmarking and Validation	190

CHAPTER 20: ADVANCED HANDS-ON EXERCISES — 191

Network Penetration Testing — **191**

Planning a Penetration Test	191
Establishing Test Environment	192
Footprinting Targets	192
Vulnerability Analysis	193
Active Attacks	193
Reporting and Remediation	193

Digital Forensics and Incident Analysis — **194**

Planning and Preparation	194
Initial Response	194
Eradication and Recovery	195
Validation and Reporting	195
Strengthening DFIR Skills	195
Red Team vs. Blue Team Exercises	196
Planning	196
Blue Team Preparation	196

Red Team Operations — **197**

Exercise Scenarios	197
Lessons Learned	197
Expanding Scoping and Complexity	198
Conducting post-exercise Hotwashes and Tabletops	198
Documentation and Reporting	198

CONCLUSION — 200

APPENDICES — 202
Glossary of Cybersecurity Terms — **202**
Recommended Tools and Software — **207**
Sample Security Policy Templates — **207**

INTRODUCTION

Welcome to The Cybersecurity Bible, a comprehensive guide to help you master cybersecurity and take on leadership roles in this critical field. As our world becomes increasingly digital and interconnected, the need for strong cybersecurity defenses has never been greater. Organizations, large and small, must protect vast troves of sensitive data and complex networks from a rising tide of cyber threats. At the same time, security professionals are in high demand to safeguard systems and enable our digital way of life.

We live in an increasingly connected world, with nearly every aspect of our personal and professional lives now facilitated through internet-enabled devices and digital systems. This hyper-connectivity has led to unprecedented efficiency, convenience, and capabilities - but it has also exposed us to new risks. As our reliance on technology grows, so does our vulnerability to cyber threats that can disrupt critical systems, expose sensitive data, and inflict financial damage.

Cyber-attacks are growing more frequent, sophisticated, and devastating each year. A 2022 report found that cybercrime now costs the world over $6 trillion annually - making it the third-largest economy after those of the United States and China. No organization, large or small, is immune - everyone from multinational corporations to hospitals, schools, and local municipalities has fallen victim. As connectivity expands into practically every consumer product through the Internet of Things (IoT), our risk exposure widens even further. Even individuals now face threats like ransomware, identity theft, and online fraud on a routine basis.

It's clear that cybersecurity has become pivotal to the functioning of the modern world. Organizations are scrambling to ramp up protections and respond to incidents. There is now incredible demand for cybersecurity talent to take on critical roles defending networks, data, and operations.

As a veteran technology professional who has designed, built, and secured networks for over 15 years, I've witnessed this mounting cyber threat firsthand. I've handled my fair share of attempted infiltrations, sifted through logs to identify anomalies, and assisted clients in recovering from attacks. I've also seen the severe disruptions organizations face when they lack proper safeguards - costing them millions in damages along with their customer's trust.

It was this backdrop that motivated me to write The Cybersecurity Bible. As cyber risks compounded, I kept encountering knowledge gaps even among seasoned security professionals. Many have deep expertise in one domain like networking or compliance but little visibility into others like application security or incident response. This limited perspective makes it difficult to contain sophisticated threats that span multiple domains. Even worse, those new to the field lack a structured curriculum to develop well-rounded competencies.

There was a glaring need for an authoritative volume that covered the full spectrum of cybersecurity in technical detail. A "bible" that consolidated everything industry practitioners need to know - laying out foundational concepts along with the latest defenses, tools, and best practices. One that not only explains key principles but facilitates hands-on skill-building through real-world exercises. And importantly, one that prepares readers to provide visionary leadership as our digital infrastructure grows in complexity.

I designed The Cybersecurity Bible to fill this need, equipping readers with comprehensive mastery of the field through five sections:

Book 1 covers the Fundamentals, getting readers up to speed on core concepts like risk management, security policies, legal issues, and the CIA triad of confidentiality, integrity, and availability that underpins information security.

Book 2 dives into Network Security, revealing how to design, implement, and monitor network architectures with maximum security. Readers explore essential protections like firewalls and encryption while also building skills to detect and respond to live threats against infrastructure.

Book 3 focuses on application security - arguably the most frequently exploited attack vector today. Readers will lock down web apps, harden databases against data exposures, and secure emerging technologies like cloud computing and the Internet of Things.

Book 4 takes the lens of Endpoint Security and User Awareness. Readers will master strategies to secure employee devices, train staff to spot phishing lures and comply with complex security regulations.

Finally, Book 5 prepares readers for senior Leadership Roles driving enterprise security strategy. We cover building security teams, managing high-stakes incidents, nurturing organizational culture, and running sophisticated red team exercises to stress-test defenses.

Each section features hands-on labs allowing readers to directly hone skills like threat hunting, penetration testing, and digital forensics against simulated networks modeled after real-world systems. By working through over twenty virtual scenarios, you'll gain the experience needed to succeed as an in-demand cybersecurity pro.

Supplementing the hands-on content are hundreds of figures, tables, and code samples illustrating complex concepts along with case studies demonstrating applied defenses against actual attacks. I also synthesize insights from my extensive industry experience securing critical infrastructure into easy-to-adapt policies, procedures, and best practices.

While cyber threats will undoubtedly grow in unpredictability and impact, the future needs cyber warriors ready to stand vigilant. Whether a lifelong IT professional or an aspiring expert, The Cybersecurity Bible delivers the structured curriculum you need to master this indispensable domain. By the end, you'll be armed with versatility across security domains, situational experience from labs, and leadership acumen to spearhead teams protecting our digital assets.

Remember - dynamic systems fail without properly engineered safeguards in place. As connectivity spreads, the expertise within these pages makes the difference between a world that's vulnerable and one that's secure. I invite you to join me on this journey to the front lines of cyber defense!

BOOK 1
Fundamentals of Cybersecurity

CHAPTER 1
Cybersecurity Basics

Defining Cybersecurity

With the increasing reliance on technology and digitalization across all spheres of life, cybersecurity has become one of the most important issues in the modern world. While technology has opened up numerous benefits and opportunities, it has also introduced new risks and vulnerabilities that can be exploited by cybercriminals, hackers, and hostile entities. As more and more sensitive data and critical systems move online and get connected, it becomes imperative to implement robust cybersecurity measures. However, before understanding the need for cybersecurity and its various aspects, it is first important to clearly define what cybersecurity actually means.

WHAT IS CYBERSECURITY?

At its core, cybersecurity refers to the collection of tools, policies, security concepts, safeguards, and practices that are aimed at protecting computers, networks, programs, and data from damage, unauthorized use, or attack. In simple terms, it can be defined as measures taken to protect the information systems of an individual user, organization, or government from cyber threats. These threats can include anything from malware and hacking to phishing scams and data breaches. Cybersecurity ensures confidentiality, integrity and availability of information and information systems by anticipating, preventing, detecting, responding to, and recovering from cyber-attacks. It takes into consideration not only threats from hackers but also issues of privacy, lawful interception, intellectual property theft, and much more. Cybersecurity aims to address risks related to information stored on technologies, the technologies themselves, and the use of those technologies for the continuation of business/operations. Overall, it works to establish security measures to protect the entire digital ecosystem, including hardware, software, networks, programs, data, and users.

SOME KEY RESPONSIBILITIES OF CYBERSECURITY

Given its broad scope, cybersecurity encompasses a variety of responsibilities, including:

Risk Management: It involves identifying and assessing cybersecurity risks to systems, networks, and assets and then determining acceptable risk levels and appropriate risk mitigation strategies.

Asset Management: It requires keeping an updated inventory of cyber assets like hardware, software, data, etc., and establishing ownership and protection requirements for each.

Access Control: It aims to restrict access to authorized users only and prevent unauthorized use, modification, or destruction of assets. It includes user identification and authentication via techniques like passwords, biometrics, etc.

Data Security: It deals with the classification, handling, storage, and transmission of data according to sensitivity to ensure confidentiality, integrity, and availability. It applies measures like encryption.

Compliance: It aims to ensure adherence to relevant security policies, baseline standards, procedures, and legal or contractual obligations.

Awareness and Training: It encompasses security awareness programs and training initiatives to sensitize users about cyber threats and best practices.

Incident Response: It involves preparation, detection, analysis, mitigation, and lessons learned from and reporting cybersecurity incidents.

Monitoring and Evaluation: It keeps track of systems and events through logging and continuous vulnerability monitoring. Metrics are used to assess security effectiveness and drive improvements.

SCOPE AND DOMAINS OF CYBERSECURITY

Given its all-encompassing nature in today's digital era, cybersecurity can apply across several domains, including:

Infrastructure Security: It deals with protecting physical network components, data centers, communication mediums, and support systems from threats. This includes locking down routers, switches, firewalls, etc.

Application Security: It focuses on embedding security features into applications at the coding and architecture level against vulnerabilities, bugs, and weaknesses.

Cloud Security: With the increasing usage of public and private cloud infrastructure and services, it manages security risks in cloud computing models of software, platforms, and infrastructure as a service.

IoT Security: The massive proliferation of internet-connected devices like sensors and appliances requires securing this ecosystem of interconnected "things" against botnets and other cyber-attacks.

Mobile Security: Due to the enormous mobilization of activities on smartphones, tablets, and smartwatches, this domain involves securing such personal devices, applications, and networks.

End-point Security: It aims to harden security on end-user systems like desktops, laptops, etc., through measures like antivirus, firewalls, encryption, and patch management.

Information Security: By safeguarding critical data along with related people, processes, and technology used to handle that data, it governs the security of crucial databases, backups, and records.

Operational Security: It focuses on ensuring the safety of operational processes, change management, backups, disaster recovery, and incident response to minimize disruptions.

Industrial Control System Security: Critical infrastructure sectors rely on industrial control systems that manage utilities, production, and transportation. Their security is paramount.

Organizational Security: High-level strategies, policies, awareness programs, staff training, budgeting, audits, reporting, etc., help create an organizational culture of security

The CIA Triad: Confidentiality, Integrity, and Availability

For ensuring cybersecurity and protecting information, one of the foundational concepts that is still widely used today is the CIA triad. It lays down three crucial tenets of information security - confidentiality, integrity, and availability, abbreviated as CIA. Together, these principles address key facets related to controlling access to information resources and systems while upholding their reliability and usability. Adhering to the CIA triad helps safeguard digital assets and tackle basic cybersecurity requirements.

CONFIDENTIALITY

The first principle of the CIA triad is confidentiality, which refers to limiting access to information only to authorized users. It prevents intentional or accidental access, modification, or disclosure of information to unauthorized individuals. Confidentiality aims to protect the privacy of data by restricting information access on a need-to-know basis.

Some key methods to achieve confidentiality include:

Access Controls

Mechanisms like authentication, authorization, and accounting help ensure that only verified and approved users can view or use data through techniques like unique user credentials, permissions, cryptographic keys, etc.

Encryption

Conversion of data into an unreadable coded format during storage or transmission helps maintain privacy and prevents disclosure even if the encrypted data is accessed illegally. Popular algorithms include AES, 3DES, RSA, etc.

Authentication

Verifying user identity through passwords, biometrics, digital signatures, smart cards, etc., before granting access establishes the right to view or change information.

Physical Security

Restricting physical access to storage devices, servers, database nodes, etc., and storing sensitive data avoids loss of possession, which may compromise confidentiality.

Awareness Training

Educating users about their responsibilities in classifying and handling data as per sensitivity prevents accidental exposure through ignorance.

Firewalls

Network layer protection devices like firewalls filter inbound and outbound network traffic to block unauthorized access while permitting legitimate communications.

Data Loss Prevention

Technologies that discover, monitor, and protect sensitive data leakages across file transfers, web, email, and removable media help ensure confidentiality.

Privacy Laws

Adhering to privacy legislation while collecting, storing, and using personal information establishes accountability and reassurance for individuals.

Proper confidentiality controls prevent data breaches, identity thefts, and unintentional sharing of restricted information. They form the foundation of privacy and build user trust in the handling of their personal details. Organizations must strike a balance between open access and need-to-know policies for optimal confidentiality.

INTEGRITY

The second principle of integrity relates to safeguarding the accuracy, completeness, and reliability of information, assets, and IT systems. Any unauthorized or improper modification should be prevented, and only authorized changes are carried out. Integrity ensures information trustworthiness and truthfulness.

Some measures to achieve integrity include:

Authorization: Granting access after verifying users' permission levels and rights helps restrict changes only to authenticated individuals.

Non-Repudiation: Using digital signatures and timestamps in transactions avoids denial of performed actions by binding users to their conducted operations.

Input Validation: Checking incoming data format and values against expected specifications filters improper values at entry points.

Audit Logs: Detailed logging of system and user activities helps monitor authorized and unauthorized changes for detection and recovery in case of integrity breaches.

Configuration Management: Establishing baselines, monitoring, and controlling all alterations to systems, networks, and applications through change management avoids unintended cascading effects.

Patch Management: Prompt installation of software fixes from vendors prevents exploitation of technical defects compromising integrity due to known vulnerabilities.

Malware Detection: Use of antivirus, intrusion prevention, and other tools identifies and eliminates malware that may corrupt files, partition tables, or alter logic.

Media Sanitization: Secure erasure or destruction of storage media like hard disks prevents unintentional exposure or reuse of previous data, compromising the integrity of new information.

Regular integrity checks coupled with version control and rollback capabilities are essential for trust in data accuracy and authenticity of transactions in the digital world. Compromised integrity severely undermines credibility.

AVAILABILITY

The third principle, availability, signifies uninterrupted and timely access to systems and data by legitimate users whenever required. Denial of availability amounts to information loss, affecting normal functioning and productivity. It ensures the reliability of service delivery.

Some best practices for availability include:

Redundancy: Maintaining duplicate components like servers, network links, power supplies, etc., ensures continuity amidst single-point failures through fail-over or load balancing capabilities.

Capacity Management: Adequate sizing of IT infrastructure and bottleneck identification/resolution activities meet future demands without performance degradation.

Prevention of Distributed Denial of Service (DDoS) Attacks: Mechanisms like reverse proxies, rate-limiting, and bandwidth throttling stop the flood of artificial traffic from overloading targets.

Business Continuity Planning: Establishing fallback procedures, alternate processing sites, backups, and disaster recovery drills minimizes disruptions from disasters or emergencies.

Preventive Maintenance: Regular health checks, software updates, and hardware servicing extend system/component lifecycles and catch potential faults in advance.

Incident Response Planning: Guidelines for immediate containment and long-term resolution of security breaches restore services expeditiously.

Vulnerability Management: Timely patching, configuration hardening, and security monitoring address vulnerabilities before exploitation impacts availability.

Access to Alternate Channels: Providing multiple communication channels like email, portal, and contact centers diversifies points of failure.

Change Management: Proper planning and testing of alterations avoids unforeseen downtime due to configuration errors.

Maintaining optimal availability levels is crucial for uninterrupted experience, revenue protection, regulatory obligations, and business continuity amid disruptive events. Downtime can prove severely costly and damage the brand's reputation.

EVOLUTION OF THE CIA TRIAD

Proposed in the 1980s by authors like Arthur W. Salle and Roger A. Grimes, the CIA triad has remained a fundamental information security concept for over three decades, providing a clear framework to tackle cyber threats. However, with advancements in technologies, threats, and regulations, it has also evolved over time:

CIA Plus One: Additional principles like authenticity and non-repudiation were introduced to address digital forgeries and online transactions.

Confidentiality, Integrity, Availability, and Accountability (CIAA): Accountability was added for compliance with expanding privacy laws around monitoring user activities and ensuring responsible practices.

Confidentiality, Integrity, Availability, Maintainability, Manageability (CIAMM): Maintainability refers to keeping controls running optimally, while Manageability focuses on overseeing policy enforcement and reporting.

Confidentiality, Integrity, Availability, Resiliency (CIAR): Resiliency signified the ability to continue critical functions under cyber-attacks through tolerance and rapid recovery capabilities.

Confidentiality, Integrity, Availability, Authenticity, Non-repudiation, Accountability, Privacy: Emerging principles of authenticity, non-repudiation, accountability, and privacy added new dimensions to cyber risk evaluations.

The CIA triad still serves as a core concept, while most frameworks now converge on seven high-level domains of computer security, including Confidentiality, Integrity, Availability, Authentication, Authorization, Accountability, and Assurance. Continuous extensions have kept it relevant with changing threat landscapes.

IMPLEMENTING THE CIA TRIAD

The practical application of the CIA triad requires assessing information sensitivity, identifying valuable assets, and mapping them to existing and potential risks. Organizations must:

- Classify data based on levels of confidentiality, integrity, and availability required during usage, storage, and transmission.

- Apply appropriate technical and administrative controls catering to classification and risk exposure to establish baselines.

- Monitor adherence through compliance audits, vulnerability assessments, penetration testing, and regular reviews.

- Train users regarding acceptable usage policies and the importance of basic security hygiene for CIA support.

- Upgrade existing protections and plug control gaps based on evaluation outcomes and new threat insights.

- Maintain continuity through disaster recovery drills, backup testing, and redundant secondary systems.

- Get executive sponsorship for adequate security budget and resources to strengthen CIA posture proactively.

- Following a CIA-based risk management framework in designing and operating organizational systems helps meet basic security needs effectively and build resilience against cyber threats.

Common Cyber Threats

With the proliferation of devices, online activities, and digital data, cyber threats have become commonplace in today's interconnected world. As cyber criminals continuously evolve their tactics, identifying prevalent threats is crucial for organizations to assess risks and prioritize defenses.

MALWARE

One of the most pervasive threats is malware - a general term for various malicious software designed to infiltrate systems without consent. Some common malware types include viruses, worms, Trojans, etc. Viruses attach themselves to legitimate programs/files and replicate, potentially damaging data or systems during spread. Worms also self-propagate across networks, exploiting security vulnerabilities, but do not require separate files to exist. Trojans disguise as legitimate software to gain access for illicit activities like data theft or installing additional malware payloads. Other malware conducts distributed denial of service attacks, collects passwords/financial details, or modifies system configurations to interfere with functioning. Polymorphic malware changes signatures to evade detection while still delivering payloads. Zero-day exploits targeting unknown vulnerabilities pose advanced risks. Organizations should implement multilayer defenses, including endpoint protection, firewalls, patching, and user awareness.

RANSOMWARE

A malicious software variant holding data hostage until ransom is paid is ransomware. It employs encryption or locks users out until payment. Some encrypt files and demand cryptocurrency, while others threaten to delete sensitive data entirely if not paid. Ransomware developers continuously improve evasion techniques while ransom amounts increase. WannaCry and NotPetya caused massive disruptions worldwide using exploits allowing lateral movement within networks. Ransomware prevention requires diligent patch management, backups, access controls, and user education against clicking suspicious links or opening unverified attachments. Having incident response plans aids recovery without paying ransoms, which may still not guarantee data returns.

PHISHING AND SOCIAL ENGINEERING

Deception techniques to steal sensitive information are rising threats. Phishing involves spoofing legitimate entities through emails or websites hosting malware payloads. Targets are lured into providing credentials, financial details, personally identifiable data, or clicking malicious links. Similar deception through phone calls, text messages, or social media conversations comes under vishing and smishing, respectively. Pretexting fools users into giving data by assuming fake roles/scenarios. Baiting places enticing files/links for harvesting victim details. These social engineering methods often precede other attacks and need vigilant user awareness along with spam filtering, domain validation, and multi-factor authentication.

IDENTITY THEFT

Once sensitive personal data is compromised, it fuels identity theft crimes. Stolen credentials, financial accounts, healthcare/insurance records, or social security numbers are misused for opening unauthorized accounts, filing fraudulent tax returns, obtaining medical services, or taking loans. Victims face damaged credit ratings, legal penalties, or expenditures to clear their names. Enterprises must implement proper access controls, encrypt personally identifiable data, and promptly notify customers of any breaches as required under laws. Individuals also need to practice safety habits like password hygiene and shredding documents containing private details.

HACKING

Motives behind system hacking vary from data stealing, intellectual property theft, and espionage to system sabotage or just the thrill of conquering challenges. Attackers probe networks for vulnerable services/endpoints using tools like Nmap and Metasploit, then remotely access systems through the exploitation of security holes. Privilege escalation obtains higher-level access for wider impact. Hackers may also install backdoors for long-term access. Comprehensive patch management, along with network monitoring and user training, helps avert hacking risks. Incident response skills aid damage containment. Enforcing the principle of least privilege and multi-factor authentication strengthens overall protection.

DISTRIBUTED DENIAL OF SERVICE (DDOS) ATTACKS

Overwhelming networks/services with artificial traffic volume to deny access to legitimate users characterize DDoS attacks. Attackers amass armies of infected

Internet of Things or compromised devices called botnets for launching large-scale distributed attacks. Victims include banks, government agencies, and commercial websites. UDP floods, TCP SYN floods, and HTTP floods are prevalent techniques. DDoS mitigation requires fortifying infrastructure, identifying abnormal traffic patterns, and filtering spoofed IP source addresses during events. Botnet infection prevention also plays a role through user awareness and device hardening measures.

INSIDER THREATS

With authorized access to systems and data, insiders present unique risks. Accidental leakage due to a lack of security protocols or deliberate misuse by disgruntled employees/contractors for data theft, sabotage, or espionage endangers organizations. Strict access controls based on need-to-know limit attack surfaces. Ongoing user training reinforces acceptable usage policies, while security controls like DLP help detect anomalies in information access, transfer, or modifications. Account monitoring and restriction of privileged access circumscribe insider activities.

SUPPLY CHAIN ATTACKS

Modern operations significantly rely on third-party vendors and outsourced services, creating potential entry points. Attackers infiltrate supplier networks to access bigger targets more stealthily by abusing trust relationships. Software supply chain compromises are rising threats as updates introduce backdoors unknowingly. The SolarWinds incident highlighted dangers, disrupting multiple governments through a single vendor breach. Organizations should vet suppliers, monitor third-party access rigorously, and filter external communications. Software development lifecycle security also protects against malicious inserts.

CLOUD SECURITY BREACHES

Pervasive cloud adoption brings agility, but attack surfaces have grown exponentially. Misconfigurations expose resources and migrating on-premise flaws detriments availability/integrity. Insecure interfaces/APIs allow unapproved access. Shared infrastructure risks isolating tenant environments if breached. Data breaches occur via leaked/unsecured credentials or third-party app vulnerabilities. Organizations must diligently harden cloud assets, adopt zero-trust controls, regularly review policies, and keep systems/services patched.

IOT/OPERATIONAL TECHNOLOGY ATTACKS

Billions of internet-connected "things" face inherent risks from default/Guessable credentials, vulnerabilities in outdated OS/firmware, and lack of security updates. IoT botnets like Mirai conduct DDoS attacks by enslaving cameras, DVRs, etc. Threat actors target IIoT/SCADA/ICS environments to cause physical damage by disrupting industrial processes. Strengthening device authentication, segmentation, micro-segmentation, and monitoring can help. Due to long lifecycles, air-gapping critical systems offer additional protection when possible.

WIRELESS NETWORK ATTACKS

Unsecure Wi-Fi points, implementation flaws in WPA/WPA2 protocols, and the growth of 5G expose more vulnerabilities. Hackers deploy wireless cracking tools to infiltrate networks or decrypt sniffed traffic. Rogue access points allow unauthorized entry. Improper hotspot configuration lures users into fake login pages for phishing. Regular audits identifying weaknesses, enabling encryption, and conducting policy compliance activities can prevent such wireless network breaches.

ENCRYPTION ATTACKS

Advances in code-cracking parallel evolving encryption standards. Brute-force attacks against vulnerable algorithms render obsolete protections ineffective. Quantum computing also threatens algorithms if powerful enough. Diversifying cryptosystems, increasing key sizes, and closely monitoring research help stay ahead of decryption capabilities alongside accelerated algorithm upgrades. Incident responses must assume data sensitivity even after deletion if stolen while encrypted with crackable schemes.

CHAPTER 2
Risk Assessment and Management

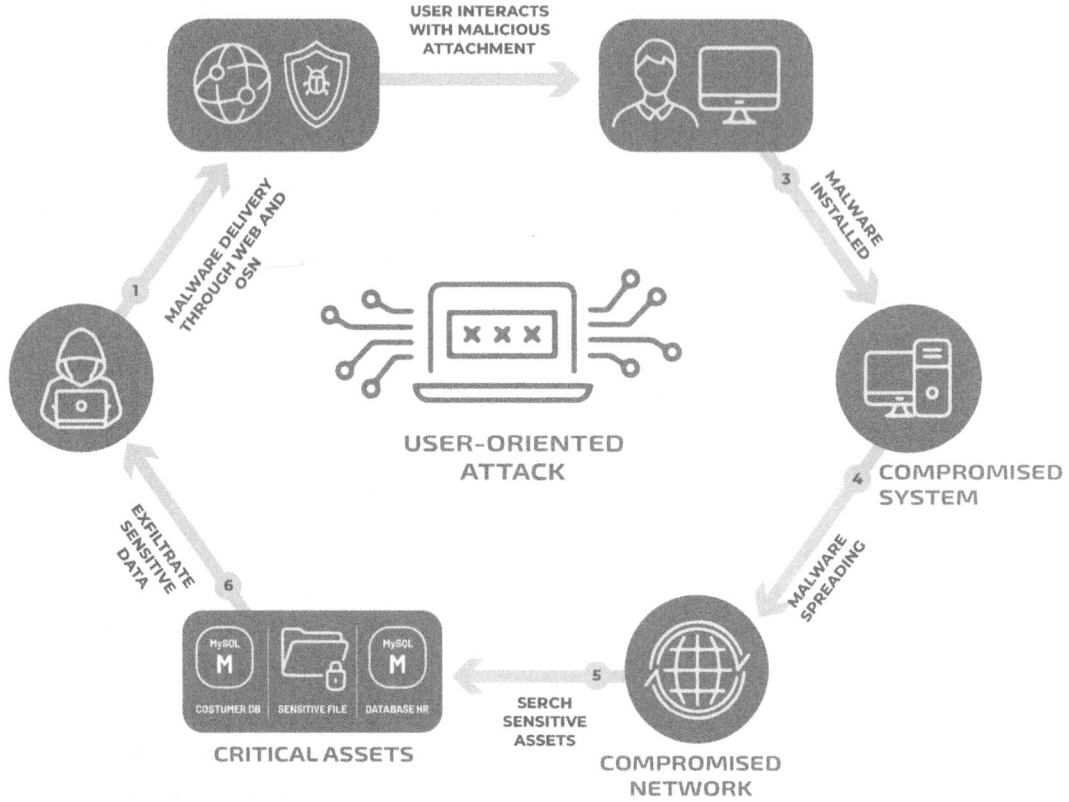

Identifying Vulnerabilities

Properly identifying vulnerabilities is the critical first step in any effective cybersecurity risk management program. Without a clear understanding of where an organization may be weak or exposed, it is impossible to assess risks accurately or prioritize mitigation strategies.

MAPPING ASSETS

To identify vulnerabilities, an organization must first map out and categorize all important assets that need protection. This process is known as asset inventory or asset management. Assets can include both digital and physical items of value to the organization, such as:

Systems and Applications

All active computer systems, software programs, mobile apps, and websites must be accounted for. Details like ownership, purpose, criticality, dependencies, configuration, patch status, and other attributes should be recorded.

Network and Infrastructure

All components that transmit or process data, including physical and wireless networks, routers, firewalls, servers, databases, and cloud systems, must be part of the inventory. Logical network diagrams mapping connections and flows of data help visualize assets and trust relationships.

Endpoints and Devices

Desktops, laptops, smartphones, IoT devices, point-of-sale systems, medical equipment, and any other endpoints on or connecting to the network should be tracked. BYOD policies complicate endpoint management and introduce further risks.

Data

All sensitive, regulated, and business-critical data stored both on-premise and off-site in the cloud requires classification in the asset inventory. This includes Personally Identifiable Information (PII), Protected Health Information (PHI), intellectual property, financial records, customer lists, and other valuable data assets.

Facilities and Physical Spaces

Buildings, offices, manufacturing facilities, warehouses, and other physical locations where technology assets or sensitive data are housed or accessed must be mapped. Items like security systems, emergency procedures, and access controls are important to understand dependencies and physical vulnerabilities.

THIRD-PARTY RELATIONSHIPS

Service providers, vendors, suppliers, partners, and other external entities that are granted access to internal networks or data through application programming interfaces (APIs) or other integrations also represent potential vulnerabilities and must be documented. Contracts and data-sharing agreements shape these third-party risks.

MONITORING ASSET INVENTORY

Keeping an up-to-date asset inventory is challenging, given the dynamic nature of today's digital environments. New systems, software, and devices are frequently procured without IT awareness. Endpoint management becomes difficult when employees use personal devices for work. Cloud services, microservices, and containers evolve code bases rapidly. As a result, asset inventories require continuous monitoring, review, and auditing to remain accurate representations of the environment. Automated discovery tools, configuration management databases (CMDBs), and asset tag scanning help asset managers scale up the management of growing attack surfaces.

MAPPING DATA FLOWS

Understanding vulnerabilities also means illuminating how data and systems interconnect within the organizational environment and beyond. Mapping data flows between assets provides crucial context for risk assessments and compliance activities. These network diagrams should capture the following:

- Interdependencies between systems, applications, and databases
- Connections to external networks, APIs, and cloud services
- Backup and disaster recovery processes
- Workflow authorizations between departments and roles
- Transmission of data to and from third parties, customers, and partners
- Transfer of physical media like backups, laptops, or printed reports
- Geographic locations where data is stored, accessed, or processed

These asset interconnections reveal opportunities for lateral movement if one system is compromised, compliance risks from unauthorized data sharing, and single points of failure. They help surface vulnerabilities around authorization controls, network segmentation, air gaps, and data protection practices during transfers.

IDENTIFYING SOFTWARE VULNERABILITIES

Software applications and operating systems contain vulnerabilities that threat actors actively seek to exploit. Vulnerability scanning and penetration testing are, therefore, critical activities in any vulnerability identification program. Automated vulnerability scanning products like Nessus, Qualys, Rapid7, and others continuously scan internal and external systems for known vulnerabilities present in applications and OS versions based on their fingerprints.

Scanning helps uncover:

1. Unsupported and out-of-date software/OS no longer receiving security patches
2. The presence of vulnerable components with public exploits available
3. Misconfigurations and unnecessary services exposed to networks
4. Default or easily guessable credentials still in use
5. Lack of encryption or weak encryption algorithms

Penetration tests build on these scans by simulating real attacks to identify vulnerabilities that may have been missed. Testing involves analyzing source code, baiting users with social engineering, attempting privilege escalation, exploiting vulnerabilities, cracking passwords, and other hacking techniques - all with the authorization of leadership. Vulnerabilities uncovered help prioritize remediation for the highest impact flaws.

IDENTIFYING CONFIGURATION VULNERABILITIES

Beyond just vulnerabilities inherent to software or operating systems themselves, improper configuration settings introduce many opportunities for exploitation. Many security incidents can be traced back to preventable configuration weaknesses if not proactively managed. Common issues include exposing insecure or unnecessary network services and ports to potential attackers instead of limiting accessibility strictly to approved applications and users. Not segregating systems through adequate logical network segmentation allows lateral movement between zones in the event of a compromise. Using default or weak credentials on core appliances like firewalls, routers, and databases bypasses integrated authentication controls. Insufficient access controls, permissions, and authorization definitions can grant more access than necessary. Unrestricted directory listings and information disclosures leaking indications of system structures and contents aid adversaries. Outdated and unpatched software versions are well-known to leave exploitable vulnerabilities.

IDENTIFYING PEOPLE VULNERABILITIES

While technology defenses protect the environment, people ultimately remain both the greatest vulnerability as well as the last line of defense. Social engineering, phishing, insider threats, and human errors create huge risks if they are not mitigated. There are several common human and process-based security risks that can undermine an otherwise technically robust protection program. A lack of security awareness or incomplete security training programs can leave employees vulnerable through phishing or unaware of their ongoing obligations to report anomalies. Unenforced or unclear policies around issues like credentials, BYOD usage, remote work equipment security, and use of social media for business purposes often result in unintended data exposures. Common mistakes like reusing passwords across accounts or writing passwords down circumvent controls. Access by separated or terminated employees also continues if IT does not properly configure identity and access management systems to automatically revoke all inappropriate accesses expeditiously according to offboarding checklists.

IDENTIFYING PROCESS VULNERABILITIES

Just as with technology and people vulnerabilities, gaps within security processes create issues.

Rigorous reviews of key organizational processes help strengthen overall security postures. Regular auditing of change, patch, and configuration management operations ensures that only approved modifications occur to critical systems through well-defined approval and testing workflows, minimizing disruptions and vulnerabilities. Evaluating incident response plans, disaster recovery procedures, and business continuity strategies helps validate preparedness through tabletop exercises identifying coverage gaps. Threat modeling within the secure software development lifecycle, along with risk management programs, aims to address vulnerabilities early. Examining identity and access management operations helps confirm the appropriate lifecycle handling of user accounts and entitlements according to the principles of least privilege.

Assessing Risk

RISK IDENTIFICATION

Brainstorming broadly combines diverse expertise, considering less obvious perspectives. Profiling characterizes threats based on motivations and capabilities. Predictive modeling factors, historical patterns, and future uncertainties. Risk inventories capture everything requiring oversight or monitoring. Documentation justifies priorities and resource allocation.

RISK ANALYSIS

Probability and impact scales remain objective yet granular enough to effectively prioritize. Qualitative assessments estimate intangible factors. Modeling simulates risk correlations and risk accumulations. Dependencies compounding single points of failure necessitate additional scrutiny. Scenarios evaluate plausible worst cases driving residual risk tolerance.

RISK EVALUATION

Recalculating introduces each new treatment to affirm viability. Cost-benefit analyses optimize selections by weighing expenditures against expected reductions. Risk attitudes mature as exposure experience grows. Emerging risks prompt reevaluation, ensuring preparedness. Oversight validates reasonableness, aligning risk evaluation consistently with objectives.

CONTROL ASSESSMENT

Control owners substantiate control suitability, implementation, and operating effectiveness. Independent validation reinforces reliability annually or for significant changes. Performance metrics evaluate deficiencies over thresholds necessitating improvement. Compliance validations consider internal policies and external regulations. Benchmarking guides continuing relevance.

TREATMENT OPTIONS

Detailed implementation plans establish ownership, milestones, dependencies, and success metrics. Change management integrates permanent solutions seamlessly. Testing validates treatments performed as designed under intended and stressful conditions. Pilot programs prove viability before wholesale adoption. Transference partners undergo qualification vetting.

POLICY AND PROCESS REVIEW

Legal and audit advisors ensure rigor, reasonableness, and documentation sufficiency. Versioning traces maturity over time. Interpretive guidance promotes consistent understanding. Templates consider organizational changes and scale. User surveys capture strengths and obstacles for optimization.

RISK MONITORING

Dashboards visually convey risk portfolio status, treatment progress, and oversight needs. Robust sensing establishes baseline behaviors and user entitlements, detecting anomalies. Issue tracking manages remediation dependencies to resolution. Customized reporting serves varying stakeholder needs.

COMMUNICATION AND TRAINING

Mandatory certifications validate comprehension and responsibilities. Reinforcements address gaps revealed through monitoring, audits, or incidents. Knowledge repositories compile institutional expertise promoting exam preparation and succession. Feedback shapes effectiveness, continually improving the program.

Risk Mitigation Strategies

ASSESSING CURRENT STATE

The first step in developing a risk mitigation strategy is gaining insight into the existing risk management practices and control posture. A review of vulnerability assessments, security policies, incident response plans, and other artifacts provides a starting point. Gaps between current and required practices are identified to focus mitigation activities.

TECHNICAL CONTROLS

One of the primary means of mitigating risks involves implementing technical controls. Ensuring systems are securely configured according to baselines reduces exploitation surfaces. Patching known vulnerabilities promptly addresses entire categories of flaws. Network segmentation limits lateral movement potential if one segment is compromised. Endpoint detection and response solutions enhance visibility and response capabilities. Data encryption protects confidentiality even if exposures allow information exfiltration. Default deny firewall rules block unnecessary inbound/outbound traffic. While vital, technical controls alone are not sufficient as human and process vulnerabilities also exist.

PROCEDURAL CONTROLS

Complementing technical controls and procedural measures helps reduce risks stemming from human and process weaknesses. Comprehensive security policies define requirements and assign responsibilities. Mandatory security awareness training educates personnel, reducing social engineering risks. Configuration management policies maintain standard system builds. Change management processes, including review and testing of updates, limit unintended issues. Segregation of duties prevents the concentration of sensitive privileges. Incident response plans outline communication and containment procedures. Processes must be clearly documented and consistently enforced.

TESTING EFFECTIVENESS

Regular security testing assesses control effectiveness and enables improvements. External penetration tests mimic real attacks, highlighting vulnerabilities before exploitation. Internal vulnerability scanning coupled with remediation validates technical configurations, and patch levels are appropriately managed over time. Phishing simulations measure understanding of current threats and social engineering techniques. Tests are most valuable when conducted frequently by independent assessors with expertise in the latest adversary tactics.

TECHNOLOGY ENVIRONMENTS

Mitigations must account for unique attributes of each environment, including infrastructure architectures, data types, and user populations. Strategies for office workstations differ from industrial control systems. Staff laptops require mobile considerations compared to mission-critical servers. Public-facing websites demand a different focus than private intranets. Tailoring controls to environment details optimizes investments.

RESIDUAL RISK ACCEPTANCE

Not all exposures can be fully mitigated given constraints. Residual risks below the organization's risk tolerance may be formally accepted if additional response costs outweigh marginal benefits. Acceptance acknowledges retained exposures and assigns oversight responsibilities. Reassessment periodically confirms that accepted risks remain manageable.

THIRD-PARTY DEPENDENCIES

Risk also stems from external service providers and suppliers. Vendor contract terms and auditing ensure adequate security of any third-party systems or data processing. Clearly defined requirements and oversight responsibilities mitigate risks from external relationships and outsourced activities.

COMMUNICATION AND TRAINING

A strategy relies on support from all stakeholders. Regular security updates communicate new threats and expected behaviors. Mandatory training programs educate staff, management, and third parties on their security responsibilities. Feedback channels facilitate continuous improvement. Personnel remains an extension of controls when properly informed of risks and equipped to contribute.

MONITORING AND IMPROVEMENT

A risk mitigation strategy is never complete as the landscape evolves. Continuous monitoring detects new vulnerabilities or deficiencies. Regular assessments validate strategy effectiveness against current risks and requirements. Lessons from incidents drive improvements. An ongoing, iterative approach optimizes posture against continually emerging threats and business changes over the long term.

THIRD-PARTY RISK MANAGEMENT

When third-party systems and services are integral to operations, risks stem beyond internal controls. Vendors and business partners introduce external vectors. Standards like NIST SP 800-53 Revision 5 recommend third-party assessments and agreements detailing security requirements. Contract language holds providers accountable for protecting data and meeting compliance objectives. Auditing verifies protections and responds to issues immediately. Clearly defining oversight responsibilities and communication channels mitigates cross-organizational risks.

DEPARTMENTAL COORDINATION

Individual business units each face unique risks requiring dedicated consideration. Bringing together stakeholders across departments facilitates consistent strategies. Representatives understand respective functions and constraints. Collaboration enables prioritizing efforts for the greatest impact across the whole organization. Special interest groups address concerns for high-value assets, like payment systems or R&D networks. Coordination optimizes resources across silos.

CRISIS COMMUNICATIONS

Even with robust strategies, residual risks remain. Successfully containing incidents relies on coordination and transparency. Designated spokespeople address public relations, while investigative teams analyze intrusions. Templates for notifying affected parties prepare responses. Tabletop exercises polish procedures and responsibilities in collaboration with legal, IT, and senior management. Rehearsing crisis plans promotes confidence to mitigate fallout.

REGULATORY COMPLIANCE

Strategies must conform to applicable laws and standards. Interpreting and operationalizing frameworks like GDPR or NIST CSF supports audits and assures diligence. Addressing the most stringent requirements accommodates multiple compliance needs and avoids gaps. Permits are acquired and maintained for security activities such as testing or background checks. Compliance secures reputation and enables marketplace participation.

CHAPTER 3
Security Policies and Procedures

Creating a Security Policy
STAKEHOLDER ENGAGEMENT

The first step is to engage relevant stakeholders to understand organizational security needs and goals. Interviews with leadership, departments, and compliance determine strategic priorities. Discussions with information owners identify critical assets requiring heightened safeguards. User input helps balance security with productivity. Stakeholder sign-off proves endorsement before launching the policy.

RESEARCH REGULATORY REQUIREMENTS

Identify applicable legal and contractual compliance mandates such as protecting privacy data, securing financial records, or meeting health standards. Research interpretive guidelines to properly implement technical, operational, and documentation requirements into the policy. Addressing all obligations secures reputation and enables marketplace participation.

ASSESS EXISTING CONTROLS

Review current security tools, configurations, and documentation to establish a baseline. Identify policy topics covered and gaps requiring new controls. Assess awareness and enforcement of existing policies to determine improvements. Gap analyses set realistic expectations for the existing control environment. Addressing known deficiencies strengthens future policy adherence.

DRAFT CONTENT

Define the policy scope and purpose upfront to set the context. Incorporate feedback from stakeholders alongside the compliance and control reviews. Clearly allocate roles and responsibilities across departments and position levels. Establish change management processes to modify the policy over time. Outline how the policy relates to other organizational policies, including incident response plans.

POLICY SECTIONS

Typical sections may address asset management, identity, and access controls, encryption, monitoring, patching, vendor risk, awareness training, change control, auditing, reporting incidents, discipline, and exception management. Tailor the level of technical detail to the intended audience, balancing enforceability with understandability. Cross-reference related policies as required to form a cohesive program.

REVIEW CYCLES

Iterative review cycles, including legal, compliance, information security, and stakeholder representatives, ensure comprehensive coverage and feasibility. Solicit volunteer user pilots for usability feedback. Incorporate revisions and obtain formal sign-off before roll-out. Plan review periods, such as annually or when triggered by significant business or compliance changes.

APPROVAL WORKFLOW

Route the policy electronically or physically through defined approval paths. Senior executives provide accountability validation before publication. Document versioning tracked in a policy management system maintains history. Establish an approval cadence balancing agility and oversight appropriate to the organizational structure.

PUBLISH AND SOCIALIZE

Define publication channels matching communication preferences. Email announcements, intranet pages, and all-hands meetings introduce the new policy. Targeted training customizes messaging by role. Set an effective date, allowing sufficient lead time. Replies confirm understanding of expectations before enforcement begins. Address questions transparently and consistently.

MONITORING AND ENFORCEMENT

Ensure continued awareness of expectations over time. Routine audits validate policy adherence while phishing simulations reinforce guidance. Investigations address reported incidents and near-misses to prevent recurrences. Enforce escalating remedies for repeat or serious violations. Continual improvement optimizes understandability and reduces non-compliance over the long term.

EVALUATE EFFECTIVENESS

Regular reviews assess the policy's influence on behaviors and control results over time. User and department head surveys measure awareness and opinions on adequacy. Reports from security tools quantify policy impact on related indicators. Refine sections as needed based on monitoring outcomes. Prove worth through quantifiable risk reduction and employee satisfaction.

STRATEGIC ALIGNMENT

The policy scope and objectives must support higher-level strategic goals and risk appetite. For example, an innovative company prioritizes enabling rapid product development over short-term security, while a financial institution emphasizes risk aversion. Policy content and exceptions balance mission needs with protecting assets commensurate to their criticality.

Enforcing Security Procedures

AUDITING COMPLIANCE

Regular reviews validate adherence to controls defined in policies and technical configurations. Automated auditing tools integrate with endpoints, networks, and applications to monitor for anomalies continuously. Periodic assessments by independent internal auditors measure compliance against benchmarks and address non-conformities. External third-party audits provide unbiased assurance for regulators and clients.

TRAINING ALIGNMENT

Security awareness programs introduce all personnel to expected behaviors. Interactive modules, videos, and simulations explain procedures in plain language. Comprehension assessments ensure understanding before access to resources. Refresher training addresses decreasing retention. Incentivized micro-learning optimizes engagement. Training effectiveness directly links to successful enforcement.

MONITORING ACTIVITIES

Logging and monitoring systems capture user and system activities for analysis. User entity behavior analytics detect unusual access patterns. Network sensors identify anomalous inbound/outbound traffic. File integrity monitoring checks for unexpected changes. Alerts trigger risk-based responses according to procedures. Automation scales oversight to large and distributed environments.

VULNERABILITY REMEDIATION

Scanning frequently identifies technical weaknesses. Tracking remediation tasks in a central repository prioritizes the highest risks. Notifying process owners secures resources for resolutions. Deadline extensions document constraints inhibiting immediate fixes. Periodic rescanning validates all issues addressed in a timely in alignment with policies. Unresolved risks undergo exception management.

ACCOUNT MANAGEMENT

Provisioning checklists guide the creation of new accounts according to the principle of least privilege. Deprovisioning procedures expedite access removal coordinated with HR. Access certifications verify that assigned privileges remain appropriate. Privilege escalations obtain approvals according to role-based approval matrices. Role changes maintain the segregation of duties. Procedures optimize access lifecycles.

INCIDENT RESPONSE COORDINATION

Defined roles coordinate containment, eradication, recovery, and lessons learned from security incidents. Checklists implement each standardized procedure. Communication plans outline external notifications. Forensic procedures preserve evidence. After action reviews identify areas meriting process refinements. Tabletop exercises improve coordination under stress.

CHANGE MANAGEMENT

Configuration changes undergo peer review and testing separation before production deployment. Back-out plans allow rollback. Documentation and approval workflows promote oversight and accountability. Release management for applications incorporates security into SDLC. Baselining validates the expected state following changes to avoid new weaknesses.

DIGITAL EVIDENCE MANAGEMENT

Retention policies address log data, backups, investigations, and litigation needs. Classification schemas organize sensitivity. Access controls restrict viewing according to legal, audit, or investigative rights. Chain of custody preserves integrity. Archiving considers storage limitations. Procedures facilitate forensically sound handling and disposal.

PERFORMANCE MANAGEMENT

Job descriptions incorporate security functions. Goals and OKRs include adherence and continuous improvement objectives. Performance discussions address conduct and responsibilities. Reward programs recognize achievements. Remediation or disciplinary actions promptly address non-compliance proportionate to severity and recurrence. Fair practices instill a commitment to procedures.

DEPARTMENTAL OWNERSHIP

Assign information assets and control owners to business units. Shared responsibility across departments facilitates coordination and advocates for security. Representatives act as Subject Matter Experts and steering committees to optimize efforts consistently enterprise-wide. Metrics evaluate department-level effectiveness, driving healthy competition.

ESCALATION MANAGEMENT

Non-compliances undergo documented coaching or escalating sanctions according to their impact. Mitigating factors like swift self-reporting influence responses. Investigations assign accountability impartially. Appeals allow deficiencies to be remediated prior to termination. Due process maintains procedural fairness while minimizing future risk exposure.

VENDOR RISK MANAGEMENT

Third-party assessments evaluate security pre-contract. Contracts establish baseline technical, operational, and reporting controls through the life of engagements. Monitoring confirms continuing alignment with internal procedures. Escalation plans remedy deficiencies or terminate unsafe relationships, protecting the brand and clients.

USER REPORTING

Anonymous feedback mechanisms encourage issue identification. Non-retaliation policies motivate assistance without fear of consequences. Awareness campaigns emphasize collective accountability for resilience. Earned trust promotes self-policing communities where individuals feel empowered and responsible for defense.

METRICS AND REPORTING

Dashboards visualize program effectiveness and deficiencies via key performance indicators. Automated alerts trigger a risk-based investigation or process improvements. Executive oversight examines progress, resource prioritization, and emerging risks. Transparency across levels sustains prioritization and sponsorship.

Incident Response Plans

The first step is clarifying terminology, such as the scope of an "incident." Definitions establish when procedures take effect versus escalating concerns through normal channels. Distinguishing incidents from regular operations provides necessary context.

ROLES AND RESPONSIBILITIES

Assigning owners for each function maintains accountability and continuity. Backups avoid single points of failure. Cross-training promotes preparedness for absences. Technical, investigative, public relations, and management roles each require skill sets. 24/7 availability and call trees to establish support coverage.

INITIAL RESPONSE

Checklists outline contained actions to isolate impacted systems, secure evidence, change credentials, and initiate monitoring. Prioritization of availability, integrity, confidentiality, and accountability guide initial containment. Notifications activate the response team for escalated coordination.

DATA COLLECTION AND PRESERVATION

Processes document details methodically without disturbing evidence. Logging configurations prioritize necessary contextual data relevant to each incident category. Scripts automate collection routines. Retention policies address storage and legal hold requirements. Integrity and chain of custody establish a forensically sound collection.

INCIDENT CLASSIFICATION

Definitions classify severity levels activating specific response procedures. Factors include regulatory reporting thresholds, affected populations, brand impact, and technical difficulty remediating. Benchmarks remain consistent over time. Automated decision trees provide initial incident contexts.

INVESTIGATION PROCEDURES

Playbooks outline investigation steps to comprehensively analyze the scope, source, vectors, and impacted systems. Databases manage case findings and document requests. Forensic imaging and memory dumps extract clues judiciously. Deconfliction with law enforcement coordinates multi-agency investigations.

COMMUNICATIONS PLANS

Templates and approvals establish consistent, factual messaging internally and externally. Proactive public statements manage rumors. Notices personally inform monitoring or response requirements for affected parties respecting privacy. Legal reviews mitigate disclosures, increasing harm.

VULNERABILITY ASSESSMENTS

Post-response reviews identify contributing technical weaknesses, process breakdowns, or training deficiencies for remediation. Testing verifies fixes and addresses root causes before case closure. Findings feed into policies and strengthen organizational resilience.

RESTORATION AND RECOVERY

Recovery plans rapidly restore the availability of prioritized systems and services. Restoration validates integrity through testing and user acceptance. Post-incident reviews documented lessons reinforce preparation capabilities and close knowledge gaps enterprise-wide.

EXERCISES AND IMPROVEMENTS

Tabletop exercises evaluate coordination with evolving scenarios. Lessons identified update processes for continuous enhancement. Automation accelerates routine response tasks. Yearly reviews with executive sponsorship ensure plan relevance against emerging threats and responsibilities over time. By clearly segmenting response activities and accountabilities, this overview establishes an organizational foundation for effectively handling unplanned incidents to safeguard operations, reputation, and legal compliance through tested, continually improving procedures. Please advise if any area requires expansion.

REPORTING AND NOTIFICATION

Procedures classify reportable incidents via predefined severity thresholds aligned to regulations and multi-agency information-sharing agreements. Approvals govern notifications to senior leadership, customers, regulators, and media. Escalation paths address emergent findings necessitating expanded communications.

TRIAGE AND PRIORITIZATION

Initial triage establishes critical indicators, including scope, impacts, and required actions to guide resource allocations. Prioritizing containment, eradication, and recovery prevents cascading impacts. Urgency drives responses balanced with care and accuracy.

FORENSIC INVESTIGATIONS

Processes govern forensic investigations and evidence handling, respecting legal and contractual requirements. Tools, workflows, and provenance track custody. Partnerships with accredited forensic firms strengthen specialized capabilities. Findings remain admissible in legal proceedings.

INCIDENT DOCUMENTATION

Templates capture methodology, timeline, key decisions, findings, and recommendations in a central repository. Versioning maintains history. Access controls preserve privacy and confidentiality. Integrity policies prevent tampering or deletion.

CSIRT COORDINATION

Relationships with peer SOCs, CERTs, and security agencies facilitate indicator sharing, deconfliction support, and joint investigations. Reciprocity strengthens overall cyber defense through information exchanges and coordinated responses.

AFTER ACTION REVIEWS

Structured facilitated discussions identify strengths, deficiencies, and lessons to improve future preparedness and resilience. Action items track preventive and corrective activities to a conclusion. Trending aids resource planning and training needs across the extended ecosystem.

METRICS AND REPORTING

Dashboards visualize IR program maturity via speed, thoroughness, compliance, customer satisfaction, and other KPIs over time. Logging ensures accountability and learning. Executive communication proves value while requesting sponsorship. Continuous benchmarking optimizes performance against adversity. By diligently cultivating collaboration, learning, and improvement, incident response planning helps organizations prepare for, manage, and recover from disruptions as resiliently as possible in service of protecting all relevant stakeholders. Evolution maintains relevance against a threat landscape in constant change.

CHAPTER 4
Legal and Ethical Considerations

Data Privacy Regulations

COMPLIANCE LANDSCAPE

Beyond initial research, an assessment of current practices helps prioritize efforts. Gaps between obligations and existing controls require addressing. Assessing location-specific nuances prevents oversights from ambiguous interpretations. Benchmarking among industry peers avoids unnecessary costs from over-compliance. Documenting the compliance program establishes accountability and continuous improvements. Designating cross-functional teams optimizes collaboration between legal, IT, security, marketing, and other stakeholders. Workflows integrate privacy into the organization's culture, respecting individuals proactively instead of reacting to violations. Executive sponsorship and allocated resources demonstrate prioritization, ensuring sustainable, value-added compliance.

PERSONAL DATA DEFINITIONS

Pseudonymization techniques reduce identifiability while retaining utility for permitted purposes. Aggregating or averaging statistics preserves analytics without identifying data subjects. Publicly available information requires distinguishing from personal data, requiring safeguards. Contractual commitments extend protections to third-party data subject to regulatory jurisdiction. Data inventories classify all attributes potentially qualifying as personal data, especially when combined or linked. Accountability requires data protection by default, even without a definitive determination of sensitivity. Individuals must comprehend data uses clearly to exercise autonomy meaningfully.

CONSENT AND PURPOSE LIMITATION

Consent mechanisms involve layered information customizing legal vocabulary for understandability without diluting substance. Children warrant parental involvement, respecting evolving maturity and digital rights. Granular controls avoid unnecessary breadth to simplify revocation and future uses requiring re-consent. Auditing validates data handling remains within the original or iteratively expanded scope over time. Consent management systems document and preserve evidence of permissions to satisfy regulators. Privacy dashboards visualize collected data and share permissions for transparency, empowering ongoing control.

DATA SUBJECT RIGHTS

Prioritization directs resources to fulfilling requests commensurate with sensitivity and legal urgency. Education reinforces continuing individual autonomy even after providing personal data. Anonymous aggregated analytics avoid reidentification risks from individual access. Templates address frequently asked questions proactively. Multi-factor authentication balances convenience and verification for privacy-sensitive disclosures. Translations overcome language barriers, broadening accessibility. Third parties receive sufficient context, fulfilling data subject requests accurately within their respective roles.

DATA INVENTORY AND MAPPING

Documentation provides protection to all connected systems and affiliates; however, data may be transferred, derived, or archived. Data dictionaries define attributes with sensitivity designations. Regular review and purging cycles remove personal data rendered unnecessary by obsolescence, updates, or expiration of permitted uses. Change management processes govern scope creep from new programs or acquisitions. Vendor risk assessments factor in third parties substantively participating in the data processing. Individuals retain visibility and control, traversing organizational boundaries based on consent and purpose.

DATA PROTECTION BY DESIGN AND DEFAULT

Privacy architects facilitate early assessments weighing innovation against responsible data handling. Workflows embed individual preferences during development, testing, and rollout. Contractors and third parties adopt organizational privacy standards contractually. Audits validate operationalizations adequately considering privacy risks, yet adaptability allows mission enablement. Education sustains culture change across departments by emphasizing dignity and empowerment over mere compliance. Interdependent data protection reinforces security, accuracy, and confidentiality objectives holistically.

DATA MINIMIZATION AND RETENTION

Reasonable necessity justifies collection, while excess risks exposure from unnecessary breaches or unlawful uses. Data dictionaries enforce field-level restrictions and expirations. Access controls revoke unneeded entitlements regularly according to legal documentation requirements and business needs. Data subject access requests inform whether data remains pertinent for original uses. Records management schedules retire personal information systematically without impacting legitimate operations or accounting. Resources optimize value from insights extracted carefully from minimized data stores.

DATA TRANSFERS AND ACCOUNTABILITY

Multi-tiered certifications prove qualified recipients share risks and responsibilities substantively for data protection. Contractual remedies motivate diligent handling internationally. Consent encompasses contemplated recipients specifically regardless of subsequent transfers. Incident response preparations formalize coordination for risks crossing borders. Vendor management integrates privacy assessments. Renewing due diligence periodically adapts safeguards proportionately over the lifecycle relationship. Dedicated support maintains individuals' rights extraterritorial.

BREACH NOTIFICATION AND RESPONSE

Simulations evaluate coordination across silos under stress. Metrics track timeliness, root causes, and resolutions. Notifications balance speed and care customized by recipients' needs. Credit monitoring, call centers, or legal advice support affected individuals directly. Remediation validates enduring fixes while reinforcing lessons across systems, processes, and cultures. Regulators receive full cooperation and transparency to validate responsible stewardship. Aggregate metrics evaluate program effectiveness over time.

Ethical Hacking and Penetration Testing

RISK ASSESSMENTS

Threat modeling incorporates adversarial perspectives to comprehensively map out attack surfaces and consequences. Quantifying likelihood and impact ratings establish test prioritization mathematically. Data classification schemas consider sensitivity and regulatory factors. External perspectives supplement internal knowledge. Dynamic reassessments address evolving situational risks. Test scores adapt to risk tolerance shifts over time. Documentation justifies resource expenditures protecting the most critical assets.

PLANNING AND APPROVALS

Change management processes integrate testing into routine improvement cycles. Contingency planning mitigates risks from interruptions or issues discovered. Non-disclosure agreements preserve sensitive findings from unauthorized exposure. Insurance policies address off-target impacts proportionate to the assessment level. Milestones track progress toward objectives. Report distribution lists determine oversight and stakeholders. Revision histories maintain full documentation for reference.

METHODOLOGY DEFINITION

Approved frameworks structure engagements consistently and comprehensively according to maturity models. Risk-based methodologies optimize resources, focusing on the highest vulnerabilities first. Automated tools standardize routine tests for efficiency. Penetration testing, red teaming, and purple teaming differentiate activities requiring unique talent, scope, or governance. Test cases incorporate defense evasion techniques mimicking advanced threats.

TESTER QUALIFICATIONS

Mentorship accelerates learning curves to expand capabilities over time. Partnerships supplement niche skills. Continuous vetting safeguards qualifications remain current. Professional associations advocate for the field, ensuring skills correlate to emerging threats. Recognition programs incentivize excellence. Knowledge libraries institutionalize expertise gained through experience.

ENVIRONMENT ISOLATION

Rulesets configure isolated networks identically for realism yet prevent lateral movement. Duplicated sensitive applications and data subsets enable comprehensive validation without exposure. Network segmentation localizes tests. Appliance-based isolation provides flexibility. Logs facilitate thorough forensic capabilities in the event of unintended impacts requiring investigation.

DISCOVERY AND EXPLOITATION

Reconnaissance actively profiles potential vulnerabilities through open-source intelligence, network scans, active directory enumeration, password cracking, and social engineering. Simulated attacks validate controls end-to-end across people, processes, and technologies. Privilege escalation attempts bypass access controls. Covert channels extract sensitive data surreptitiously. Post-exploitation persistence mimics advanced threats establishing stealthy backdoors.

REPORTING AND REMEDIATION

Reporting templates maintain structure and compliance usefulness unvaryingly over time. Automated dissemination routes findings appropriately. Versioning preserves the full methodology and findings history. Recommendations balance feasibility and control optimization. Tracking systems oversee timely remediation progress. Client Portal provides oversight and knowledge transfer. Reporting recognizes excellence across engagement participants and Asset Owners.

EXERCISES AND IMPROVEMENTS

Automated checks validate remediation addressed root causes before closing findings. Retainings incorporate lessons back into updated training, policies, and standard operating procedures. After Action Reviews capture the indispensable experience and insight for program enhancements. Externally validated certifications recognize process maturity over time. Continuous process improvement based on results, metrics, and feedback validates value and optimizations.

Reporting Security Incidents

Glossaries centralized terminology promoting consistent understanding. CSIRT classification schemes align stages for benchmarking and analytics. SLAs establish expected timeframes, holding teams accountable. Legal and compliance experts contextualize obligations. Auditable documentation stores policies for reference. Regular reviews consider emerging risks and technologies. Direct feedback captures edge cases necessitating clarification over time.

ROLES AND RESPONSIBILITIES

Cross-training expands coverage for absences with minimal continuity risks. Succession plans transfer expertise smoothly. Communication plans establish procedures and escalation criteria. 24/7 availability and priority service level objectives regulate urgency. Metrics evaluate individual and team performance against objectives. Recognition incentivizes dedication and improvements.

DETECTION TECHNIQUES

Heuristics detect abnormalities through profiling. User and Entity Behavior Analytics (UEBA) establish baselines separating anomalies from routine. Integration centralizes disparate logs for speed and accuracy. Automation accelerates analysis and notifies critical incidents according to tiers. Rulesets dynamically adapt thresholds based on trends. Forensics facilitate investigations from captured artifacts.

INITIAL RESPONSE

Checklists provide verifiable guidance under stress. Dedicated war rooms coordinate containment efficiently. Network segmentation localizes impacts. Changes address exposures methodically validated to stabilize the situation. Evidence chain of custody documentation begins immediately. Stakeholder notices inform the next actions and minimize interruptions.

CLASSIFICATION AND ASSESSMENT

Threat modeling maps attacker techniques and motivations. Vulnerability assessments expose weaknesses motivating the compromise. Regulatory considerations determine public disclosures or private resolutions. Impact analyses evaluate technical disruptions and reputation effects. Forecasting predicts proliferations requiring broad containment or monitoring.

COMMUNICATIONS PROTOCOLS

Spokespersons receive media relations training. Notices comply with contractual obligations, maintaining partner confidence. Multi-lingual and accessible formats care for diverse audiences. Records management retains communications history according to retention requirements. Versioning maintains visibility to status changes approvingly. FERPA and HIPAA safeguard protected data according to disclosures.

INVESTIGATION TECHNIQUES

Procedures govern legal evidence handling admissibility. Analytics identify affiliated events across disconnected systems. Timelining reconstructs the full kill chain according to evidence found. Partnerships leverage combined context or resources for urgent matters. Findings inform mitigations tested before reopening normal access.

REMEDIATION STRATEGIES

Planning establishes tasks, resources, milestones, and contingencies to return to normal operations sustainably. Fire drills validate playbooks under stress conditions. Tracking oversees progress, obstacles, and interdependencies. Change control manages scope changes. Configuration baselines enforce restoration integrity.

POST-INCIDENT REVIEW

Trending aids continuous optimization by associating root causes with deficiencies or existing risks manifesting. Documentation establishes institutional memory, reinforcing knowledge transfer. Surveys capture stakeholder feedback on experiences, allowing servicing relationships. Recognition awards excellence throughout responses and enhancements.

BOOK 2
Network Security

CHAPTER 5
Network Security Fundamentals

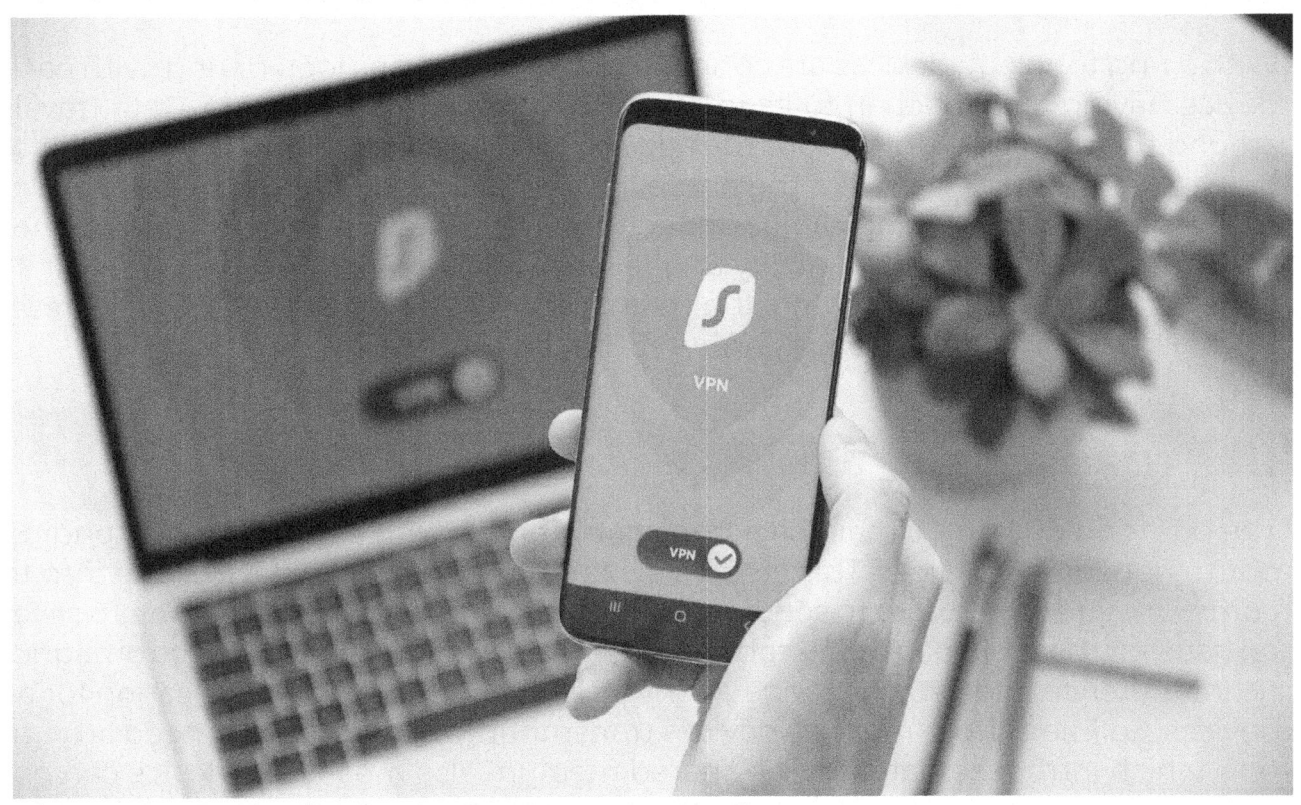

Network Topologies

A network topology refers to the geometric arrangement or layout of different components that make up a computer network. Understanding network topologies is important for cybersecurity as it helps determine how threats can spread and provides the necessary context for designing secure network architectures. This section will examine the most common network topologies in detail.

STAR TOPOLOGY

The star topology is one of the simplest configurations where each networked device connects directly to a central hub or switch. In a physical star setup, all devices are wired back to a centralized multi-port hub or switch. Logically, the arrangement is the same with devices connecting to a central device, even if they are wireless. Some key advantages of the star topology include easier troubleshooting since all connections terminate at one point, and a single-point failure does not disrupt the entire network. Devices can still communicate even if the central switch fails. However, this centralized component becomes a bottleneck and a single point of failure. If the switch is compromised, the attacker gains access to all connected devices.

RING TOPOLOGY

With a ring topology, devices are connected in a continuous loop or ring, with each device having a connection to its immediate neighbor on each side. Data travels around the ring in one direction from device to device until it reaches its destination. If one connection breaks, the entire loop is disrupted. While simple to implement physically by running cable connections in a closed loop, this topology is not widely used today due to scalability and reliability issues. A single break can halt all communication around the ring. It also introduces latency, as traffic has to travel through multiple hops to reach endpoints on the other side of the ring.

BUS TOPOLOGY

The bus topology runs a main backbone cable or bus with connections extending out to networked devices. This creates a shared medium that devices tap into to communicate. While easy to set up and extend, the bus topology is prone to several issues. If the main backbone cable is cut, the entire network fails. Electromagnetic interference and cable damage at any point can disrupt communication for all devices. Collisions from multiple devices transmitting simultaneously need arbitration, which introduces latency. The shared medium also means any device can potentially snoop on all traffic. For these reasons, the bus topology fell out of favor for wiring closet networks as switches provided more robust alternatives. However, it continues to see use in some specialized applications involving wireless networks.

MESH TOPOLOGY

A mesh topology allows for multiple redundant connections between networked devices. Any device can connect directly to any other device on the network, creating a fully connected mesh. This offers reliability through alternate paths if one connection fails. It also increases overall network bandwidth through concurrent transmissions along different links. However, complexity increases significantly as the number of devices grows due to the number of direct connections required between each pair of endpoints. Scalability becomes an issue, and the fully meshed design means more points of failure. While common for wireless mesh networks that self-configure connections, wired mesh topologies see limited enterprise use except in special applications requiring redundant connectivity.

TREE TOPOLOGY

The tree topology combines elements of the star and bus layouts into a hierarchical structure. It has a root node typically implemented as a switch or router that branches out into sub-trees. These sub-trees continue branching to form successive layers with endpoints as leaves at the far ends. The layers can be deeply nested to connect a large number of devices. Core switches sit at the top layer, with distribution and access switches forming lower sub-trees. This topology scales well as networks grow and maintain throughput through segmentation. However, failure at higher layers like the core switch can isolate large sections. Traffic must also transit multiple hops between endpoint layers. Modern enterprise networks commonly use a hybrid tree/mesh structure for segmenting traffic and providing resiliency.

HYBRID TOPOLOGIES

In practice, most large computer networks will use a hybrid topology that combines elements from multiple logical layouts depending on specific routing requirements, growth plans, and resiliency needs. For example, a core portion may follow a fully meshed design between top-tier switches for redundancy, while access switch connectivity adopts a hierarchical tree structure. An important cybersecurity consideration with hybrid approaches involves understanding the topology types used within different network segments and how threats could propagate between them. Overall, topology design plays an important role in building a secure network architecture and influencing security controls, incident response, and troubleshooting effectiveness.

WIRELESS TOPOLOGIES

While wired topologies constitute the foundation of most networks, wireless connectivity introduces its own topological considerations. Wireless access extends through the use of radio signals broadcast over the air rather than physical cables. This shared medium paradigm brings unique security issues.

INFRASTRUCTURE MODE

Most commonly, wireless networks operate in infrastructure mode, where wireless devices connect to centralized access points that bridge them to the wired network topology. The access points take the place of dedicated switches to terminate connections in a star topology. Nearby wireless clients discover and authenticate with the closest access point. This generates a number of mini-cells, with each access point essentially acting as a mini-star center. While convenient, the density of access points needs planning to avoid overlaps that weaken signals. Roaming between cells as clients move also introduces hand-off risks.

AD-HOC MODE

Ad-hoc or peer-to-peer wireless networks directly connect devices without an intermediary access point. This generates an ever-changing mesh topology as portable clients move in and out of range. While offering spontaneous connectivity, the lack of centralized management makes it difficult to enforce policies and detect risky devices. With open authentication, adversaries can more easily join the network and compromise other nodes through man-in-the-middle attacks. However, ad-hoc wireless sees some use for lightweight connectivity in IoT environments due to simplicity.

HYBRID WIRELESS-WIRED

Most real-world network topologies blend wireless and wired segments. Wireless extends access into remote areas or provides mobile clients connectivity back to the main wired infrastructure. This generates a hybrid tree topology with wired backbone layers branching into wireless sub-trees supported by access points. Understanding how devices roam between wireless cells while maintaining connectivity to the core wired network helps discern attack paths and design security zones. Authentication and traffic filtering systems need interoperability across the transition boundaries.

Encryption and VPNs

ENCRYPTION

Encryption utilizes cryptographic techniques to encode information in such a way that only authorized parties can access it. This fundamental mechanism underlies many security controls for both data protection and privacy. At its core, encryption works by using a cryptographic algorithm and encryption key to scramble information so it appears as unintelligible gibberish without the means to decrypt it. When implemented correctly and managed securely, encryption can reliably help protect sensitive network communications and stored data from unauthorized access or modification.

Encryption Algorithms

Common encryption algorithms include AES (Advanced Encryption Standard), 3DES (Triple Data Encryption Standard), Blowfish, and RSA. AES is typically the preferred choice today as it provides the strongest security with reasonable efficiency on modern hardware. The algorithm uses a variable key length of 128, 192, or 256 bits to encrypt blocks of data with 10, 12, or 14 rounds, respectively. 3DES applies the DES cipher algorithm three times for each block and is approved for backward compatibility but has known weaknesses exploited less by AES. Blowfish remains popular due to its patent-free status and high speed, yet offers lesser protection compared to AES. For asymmetric encryption, RSA excels at tasks like digital signatures and public key exchange. Choosing a robust, peer-reviewed algorithm with a large enough key length prevents current brute force decryption.

Encryption Keys

The strength of encryption ultimately derives from secure key management. A key generated using poor randomness or stored improperly poses vulnerabilities, negating the mathematical protection of even the strongest algorithms. Key lengths must exponentially increase to counter brute force attacks, leveraging advances in computing power over time. Key exchange and storage, therefore, demand sound processes based on pertinent security standards. Public key infrastructure helps automate key distribution at scale through third-party digital certificates. Robust encryption demands well-planned, audited key lifecycle operations to withstand attacks on this often-neglected yet critical component.

Encryption Use Cases

In networking, encryption plays a key role for data in transit. Transport Layer Security (TLS) - the successor to Secure Sockets Layer (SSL) - creates authenticated, encrypted connections between devices using digital certificates and session keys negotiated at startup. Widely deployed across web, mail, and other internet communications, TLS establishes an encrypted virtual channel within the underlying transport protocol like TCP. Applications can then transmit data securely over the encrypted connection without the risk of eavesdropping. IPSec provides encryption, authentication, and security associations at the IP layer, enabling Virtual Private Network (VPN) tunnels between gateways. SSL/TLS further encrypts traffic passing through these tunnels for additional safety. While older protocols like PPTP have weaknesses, newer IPsec and SSL VPN solutions harden remote access when configured correctly.

VIRTUAL PRIVATE NETWORKS

A virtual private network (VPN) establishes an encrypted tunnel between two private networks or devices to traverse an unsecured or untrusted network like the public internet securely. It logically extends a private LAN over the shared infrastructure by encapsulating traffic and tunneling it securely peer-to-peer. Common VPN protocols include IPsec, OpenVPN, and legacy PPTP.

Site-to-Site VPNs

Site-to-site or gateway-to-gateway VPNs connect entire networks securely by deploying VPN gateways or firewalls at each end of the tunnel. This allows branch offices or data centers to communicate transparently privately as an extension of the main internal network. Gateway VPNs provide scalability and simplify administration challenges of remote access VPNs involving many individual devices. IPsec dominates for site-to-site VPNs.

Remote Access VPNs

Remote access VPNs enable single devices to securely access internal networks when working remotely. Employees use VPN clients to establish an encrypted tunnel back to on-premise VPN gateways or cloud-hosted VPN services. Typical deployment involves VPN clients built into operating systems or downloadable software packages. SSL and OpenVPN work best for remote user scenarios on diverse platforms. Split tunneling routes only specified private traffic over the VPN while leaving public traffic untreated for optimized performance.

Hybrid Access VPNs

Due to increased user mobility, hybrid access VPN models that combine remote user and site-to-site connectivity have grown in popularity. They leverage cloud-based gateways accessible globally with zero-configuration native VPN clients. Hybrid VPNs balance strong security with streamlined connectivity across users, locations, and devices through a centralized interface. SSL/IPsec hybrid VPN solutions simplify network extension and remote access administration at scale. In general, VPN technology continues to advance through secure, ubiquitous access, simplified deployment models, and optimized performance even over constrained links. Well-configured encryption remains a mainstay for establishing private connections that follow security policy over unmanaged infrastructure on the path between entities. VPNs reinforce network segmentation while easing the connectivity demands of modern hybrid work environments.

Secure Remote Workflows

As remote and hybrid work models take hold, securing access to internal resources from employee-owned devices presents unique challenges. While VPNs encrypt the transport layer, additional tools strengthen overall security.

Multi-Factor Authentication

Enforcing strong multi-factor authentication (MFA) for VPN login prevents credential theft and misuse. Offering standards like OAUTH help seamlessly integrate diverse second factors like one-time passwords, security keys, or biometrics for a tightened access control posture. Prompt timeout and revocation close vulnerabilities from lost or stolen devices.

Secure Access Service Edge

Secure access service edge (SASE) consolidates network and security functions delivered as a cloud service. It can offload VPN connectivity, enforce zero-trust network access controls, and inspect encrypted traffic using inline SSL inspection powered by advanced threat protection. SASE streamlines deployment while scaling protection for globally distributed BYOD workforces.

Virtual Desktop Infrastructure

Virtual desktop infrastructure (VDI) decouples sensitive applications and data from physical endpoints by executing them remotely on centralized servers. While requiring additional infrastructure, VDI prevents data exfiltration risk in the event a device is lost or compromised. It limits what attackers can access even after infiltrating individual endpoints through malware or credential theft.

Remote Browser Isolation

For the riskiest web-based accesses, remote browser isolation launches web sessions in isolated virtual containers rather than directly on user machines. Any malware or exploits encountered get contained rather than potentially infecting corporate assets. Only screen pixels get rendered back to users, preventing harmful code from reaching endpoint systems or traversing internal networks.

Together, these emerging technologies strengthen the security posture of remote work without compromising productivity or worker experience. They add segmentation around access controls, data exposure, and execution environments to offset threats facing externally managed devices with possibly weaker safeguards than office-issued laptops. Remote access security remains critical as workforces spread across unpredictable networks and BYOD locations lacking traditional perimeter controls.

Evolving Standards

Cryptography standards regularly undergo scrutiny and revision to address new attacks. The recent move to deprecate TLS versions like 1.0 and 1.1 keeps traffic encrypted with modern cipher suites. Monitoring cryptanalysis research helps anticipate weaknesses and plan protocol upgrades proactively before threats fully materialize. Standards bodies contribute through open peer review, improving overall resilience. Companies must maintain encryption deployment currency to continue blocking network eavesdropping despite funds dedicated to cracking protocols. Testing migration impacts with TLS 1.3 adoption demonstrates an ongoing commitment to data protection. Vigilance safeguards confidentiality regardless of future decryption capabilities.

Firewall and Intrusion Detection Systems

FIREWALLS

A firewall sits at network traffic chokepoints, filtering incoming and outgoing connections based on predefined security rules. Acting as a gateway, firewalls establish a first line of defense restricting unauthorized access between networks. They operate at the network, transport, and application layers to inspect different protocol characteristics and payloads. Stateful packet inspection keeps track of communication sessions and their expected state changes, enabling dynamic responses. Modern Next Generation Firewalls integrate additional functions beyond basic packet filtering for enhanced protection.

Packet Filtering Firewalls

Early firewall generations focused on packet filtering, allowing or denying traffic through an organization's perimeter based on IP addresses, protocols, and port numbers. While simple to configure and optimize throughput, they lack visibility into actual application traffic or capabilities to modify packets. Packet filtering works well for screening basic connectivity but struggles to secure complex modern environments, relying on many dynamic application layers for productivity.

Stateful Inspection Firewalls

Stateful inspection firewalls emerged to track active network sessions, automatically allowing appropriate returning traffic dynamically. They watch the three-way handshakes establishing connections to determine the validity of return packets based on anticipated established states. Stateful inspection adds context and versatility versus rigid packet filtering but cannot fully secure applications encrypted or tunneled below the transport layer.

Next-Generation Firewalls

Leading firewall implementations combine stateful inspection with additional layers to meet evolving requirements. Application inspection identifies programs in use to enforce fine-grained policies. Advanced malware prevention scrutinizes payloads and behaviors for exploits. User identification based on IP addresses and endpoint telemetry follows individuals across devices, enforcing role-based access restrictions. Integration with proxies and VPN concentrators strengthens remote access governance. Web filtering and sandboxing augments protection for unseen content. Virtual patching bridges gaps to block emergent threats quickly. Together, these capabilities constitute robust next-generation firewall platforms that are indispensable for modern hybrid networks.

Firewall Placement

Strategically positioning firewalls protects various segments in depth. DMZ firewalls isolate external-facing systems. Core firewalls filter traffic between DMZs and internal networks. Individual internal firewalls segment business functions and contain lateral movement if breached. Network zoning establishes firewall rulesets governing movement through successive security perimeters as traffic transitions environments with differing trust postures. Bias rules toward blocking unknown traffic to enforce least privilege access aligned with business needs.

Firewall Configuration

Intent-based rule design and default-deny postures form the foundation of a strong configuration protecting vulnerabilities caused by poor change management or human error. Apply rules from most specific conditions to general cases to prevent mistakes overriding intended blocks. Regular auditing validates policy appropriateness and closes configuration weaknesses. Logging and monitoring provide visibility into rule usage, anomalies, and violations requiring further review. Configuration backups enable quick restoration from outages or unintended changes weakening posture.

INTRUSION DETECTION SYSTEMS

Where firewalls actively block unauthorized traffic, intrusion detection systems (IDS) serve as passive network sentinels, watching for signs of malicious behavior and policy violations indicating active attacks or anomalous activity. They inspect traffic at various vantage points without impeding authorized exchanges. IDS solutions analyze packets in flight as well as logs, searching for patterns or behavior signatures representing compromise indicators.

Network IDS

Network intrusion detection systems (NIDS) sit inline or tap network segments, inspecting packet payloads and headers at full line speeds without impeding performance. Monitoring ports and protocols, they detect network reconnaissance, exploits, malware callbacks, and other intrusion phases crossing network boundaries in cleartext. Traffic normalization and advanced statistical analysis help reduce false positives amid normal encrypted traffic.

Host IDS

Agent-based host intrusion detection systems (HIDS) watch individual endpoints like servers and workstations. They seek signs of local malicious behaviors, policy violations, and malware on the operating system and file levels beyond just network packets. HIDS helps spot internal infections or lateral movement remaining unnoticed at the network layer. Integrating logs from firewalls, routers, and other infrastructure aids overall detection precision.

IDS Evasion Countermeasures

Attackers study IDS systems, crafting obfuscation techniques to blend suspicious traffic with normal patterns and fly under detection radars. Techniques like fragmentation, encryption, tunneling, and protocol anomalies attempt to bypass signature detection. IDS evolves using more dynamic artificial intelligence/behavior analysis approaches robust to such evasion evolution through technique diversity, advanced correlation, and endpoint context. They serve as invaluable early indicators when adequately positioned and tuned within multilayer detection strategies.

IDS Techniques

IDS analyzes traffic and system activity using different core techniques:

- Signature Detection – Compares patterns against known threat signatures or custom rules. Effective for known exploits but misses new variants. Requires frequent signature updates.

- Anomaly Detection – Establishes baselines of normal behaviors to flag deviations that could indicate attacks. Effective for unknown threats but prone to false alarms from legitimate anomalies.

- Statistical Analysis – Applies mathematical analysis to discern behavioral patterns, finding potential intrusions amid encrypted or obfuscated traffic. Mitigates evasion but involves complex modeling prone to errors.

- Machine Learning – Systems train models on vast amounts of traffic data to automatically identify both known and new threat patterns. Effective with proper training data but can replicate unknown biases. Requires extensive computing resources.

- Log Analysis – Examines logs for irregularities across systems that could correlate with attacks. Effectively detects policy violations and lateral movement when fully integrated. It's only as good as the log data and schema.

Some IDS blend techniques to leverage respective strengths while mitigating individual limitations. Overlap between network and host sensors increases visibility when adversaries bypass one layer. Well-designed IDS remain invaluable despite imperfect accuracy due to their ability to signal potential issues requiring investigation and mitigation.

IDS Operation

IDS activation happens through either inline, passive tap, or host-based monitoring. Inline IDS sit on network links, inspecting all passing traffic while simultaneously forwarding copies to their destination. This ensures full visibility but risks impacting performance. Passive taps non-intrusively "sniff" mirrored traffic from network switches without obstructing flows. They lose visibility of unicast traffic not visible on the spanned port. Host-based agents watch individual systems without network-level context but with deeper endpoint visibility unavailable to network sensors. Detection outputs get centrally monitored and correlated for analysis. Alerts flag concerning behaviors requiring review against false positives/negatives. IDS regularly tunes detection profiles to optimize accuracy and reduce alert fatigue. Well-architected deployments provide contextual, actionable results rather than noise. Combining IDS with endpoint detection response (EDR) closes gaps to ongoing threats transiting at both network and host levels. IDS remains a pivotal partner with other tools for strengthening layered security.

CHAPTER 6
Secure Network Design

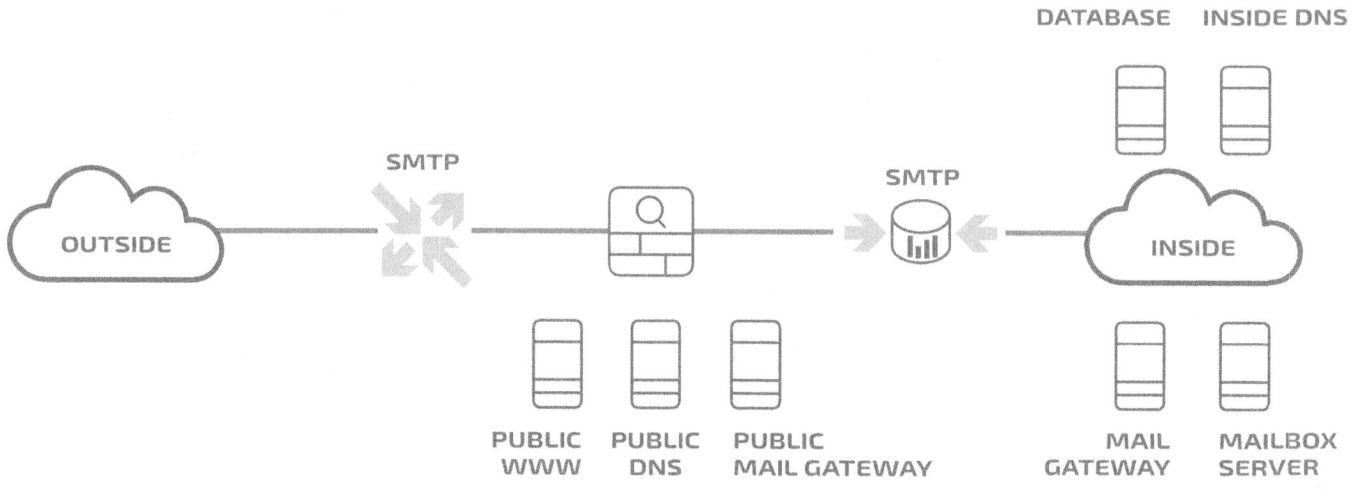

Subnetting and IP Addressing
INTERNET PROTOCOL VERSION 4

The ubiquitous Internet Protocol version 4 (IPv4) represents devices on networks with a 32-bit address written in dotted decimal notation, consisting of 4 octets or 8-bit values between 0-255 separated by periods. For example, 192.168.1.1. This offers roughly 4.3 billion possible unique addresses yet demand far exceeds this limited supply as internet adoption grew exponentially. IP addresses fulfill three main functions - uniquely identifying nodes, enabling logical addressing of systems, and facilitating routing of packets between networks. Routers directing traffic rely on network prefixes within addresses to determine forwarding paths. However, the global depletion of IPv4 address space necessitated subnetting to extend utilization from this constrained pool through network segmentation and routing.

CLASSFUL NETWORKING

The original IPv4 specification established three main network classes - A, B, and C - segmenting the 32-bit space and reserving portions for network prefixes of varying sizes. Class A allocated 8 bits to the network portion, yielding 126 networks of 16.7 million hosts each. Class B allocated 16 bits for network prefix with 16,384 networks of 65,534 hosts. Class C granted 24 bits for a network with over 2 million small networks limited to 254 nodes. While initially simple to administer, classful networking proved to be an inefficient, rigid model. Networks require dynamic sizing while predefining prefixes wastes unused host portions in smaller allocations. A transition toward classless inter-domain routing and subnetting addressed these issues through flexible exploitation of the full 32-bit address space.

SUBNETTING

Subnetting allows a single classful network to divide into multiple logical sub-networks using host portion bits normally assigned to individual systems. By borrowing bits from available host fields, an organization efficiently segments its allocated space into custom subnet sizes as needed rather than rigid classes. For example, a Class C network of 192.168.1.0/24 normally supports 254 hosts. Subnetting it as /26 carves it into two /26 networks of 62 hosts each rather than waste the unused space of a single 254-host network. Forwarding decisions now rely on the additional subnet bits enabling selective routing.

SUBNET MASKS

Subnet masks express the split between network prefix and host fields through a 32-bit value, with ones in bit positions constituting the fixed network part and zeros in the host fields available for subnet division. For a /26 subnet, the mask would be 255.255.255.192 with the first 26 bits network portion and the remaining 6 host portion bits used for subnet IDs. Proper subnet mask assignment aligns fixed network bits in masks and addresses, allowing routers to correctly interpret values to forward to intended segments. Through careful planning, subnetting optimizes the utilization of IP blocks far better than rigid classful networks.

VARIABLE LENGTH SUBNET MASKS

More advanced subnetting uses variable length subnet masks (VLSM) with discontiguous network masks to create subnets of varying sizes from a single parent network. For example, a /28, /29, and /30 subnet could coexist from one

/27 allocation. VLSM achieves maximum flexibility, though complex planning remains crucial to avoid ambiguities and challenging routers.

ADDRESS DEPLETION MITIGATIONS

As IPv4 scarcity deepened into the late 1990s, strategies emerged to counter the exhaustion, leveraging subnetting more extensively. CIDR (Classless Inter-Domain Routing) announcements standardized route aggregation through supernetting. NAT (Network Address Translation) masquerades many private devices behind public IP addresses, multiplying utilization within private subnet blocks. IPv6 completely expands the addressing space but experiences slower deployment than hoped.

SUBNET DESIGN CONSIDERATIONS

When subnetting, carefully structuring the addressing scheme avoids conflicts and allows future growth. Reserve subnet and host ranges, plan inter-subnet routing, and document clear addressing standards throughout organizations. Separate functions into logical subnets like servers, workstations, IoT, guests, and DMZs based on security posture and performance needs. Consider access requirements, fault tolerance, administrative boundaries, and capacity needs when balancing host quantities across segments. Well-designed addressing forms the network foundation upon which security and stability rely.

ADDRESSING IOT AND CLOUD

The Internet of Things skyrocketed network nodes by connecting ubiquitous sensors, appliances, and devices. Industrial control systems, city infrastructure, and consumer ecosystems all now network previously isolated systems. Cloud infrastructures dynamically allocate ephemeral addresses for transient virtual machines and containers. Such environments strain traditional addressing schemes through the sheer volume of nodes, transient relationships, and unpredictable growth patterns. New models dynamically assign temporary addresses from ISP or cloud provider pools as needed rather than static assignments. Stateful NAT464 translation enables vast IPv6 realms to coexist within IPv4 infrastructure segments through encoding.

ADDRESSING VIRTUALIZATION

Network virtualization segments cloud fabrics into isolated logical networks through overlay techniques rather than dedicated hardware. Virtual networking components like switches connect distributed virtual machine instances that are secure from each other. Overlay techniques assign hypervisor-scope IP addresses from dedicated pools separate from physical switches. Tunneling encapsulates packets between physical and virtual network tiers with network address translation mapping identities. Virtual subnets created on demand improve the mobility and scaling of transient cloud-native workloads beyond the constraints of physical networks.

ADDRESSING SECURITY

Considering network addresses hold intrinsic value as core routing identifiers, securing mechanisms like registration practices, assignment techniques, and infrastructure protocols protects their integrity. Border Gateway Protocol (BGP) inconsistencies or announcement hijacking threaten global availability through routing instability ensuing from spoofed addresses. Autonomous system number (ASN) management practices combat unauthorized announcements. Registry validation, cryptographic resource signing, and route origin authentication protocols strengthen the accuracy and resilience of inter-domain routing underpinning the internet. Overall, addressing acts as the common language enabling seamless information exchange across diverse network boundaries, necessitating robust stewardship to maintain the integrity of this critical infrastructure.

DMZs and Segmentation

NETWORK SEGMENTATION

Proper network segmentation lays the groundwork for layered security through isolating systems and trust domains. Rather than treating all devices as equal on a flat network, segmentation separates functions into logical segments restricted by capability and policy. This improves control by only permitting intended interactions and containing attacks that are unable to penetrate separate segments laterally. Core principles involve isolating public systems from internal assets to minimize exposure, separating admin/service segments from general user systems, limiting privileged access scope, dividing by function like servers, workstations, storage, guest, and IoT, and isolating production from test/development, and creating enclaves using micro-segmentation segregating applications rather than assuming host security. Technologies like routing, firewalling, VLANs, software-defined networking, and micro tunneling enable granular control over interconnected segments comprising modern hybrid networks. Combined with encryption, segmentation forms a foundational security practice protecting against worms and lateral movement.

DEMILITARIZED ZONES

The demilitarized zone (DMZ) establishes a neutral screening area between an organization's internal private network and unrestricted external internet. Systems directly exposed to threats yet requiring availability get segregated here for protection. Common use cases include web servers hosting public-facing applications and websites, mail servers for communicating outbound while screening inbound traffic, and outsourced partner systems securely exchanging data yet uncontrolled internally. Optimal DMZ design provides two firewalls, one for internal and one for external access, acting as a buffer, with no direct connectivity between DMZ and internal networks, avoiding shortcut bypass and limited internet access from DMZ systems like email and secure protocols only. Implemented correctly, DMZs enhance defenses for exposed assets through isolation from mission-critical backend systems. This reduces the impact of compromise and assists in containment should a breach occur.

SEGMENTATION DESIGN

Strong segmentation stems from a well-designed logical topology and underlying physical infrastructure properly supporting intended controls. Key factors include identifying trust boundaries between users, systems, applications, and data; enforcing ACLs at all segmentation points using firewalling, routing, and switches; avoiding single points of failure enabling north-south and east-west isolation; monitoring traffic patterns to validate policy enforcement and detecting anomalies, incorporating micro-segmentation with application-aware controls, and routinely reviewing design validity as threats evolve, and systems change. Physical constructs like redundant routers, switches, firewalls, and WiFi access points must support virtualization and micro-segmentation policy enforcement. Automated configuration, testing, and documentation streamline management at scale.

SEGMENTATION TECHNIQUES

Common means of implementing logical network divisions include VLANs, which segment switch ports into isolated broadcast domains; routing/ACLs, which filter traffic through internal firewalls restricting east-west movement; VPNs/tunnels, which isolate remote and wireless segments through encrypted connections; software-defined networking which programmatically enforce micro-segmentation policy, bastion hosts which restrict access tiers, and one-way data diodes which physically prevent certain traffic directions. Combining techniques creates a tiered maze, funneling access through successive verification layers while still enabling functionality. Defense-in-depth strengthens overall protection far beyond a monolithic flat network model.

RISKS OF POOR SEGMENTATION

Without appropriate isolation policies and controls validated through testing, interconnected systems remain susceptible to lateral intrusions leveraging initial Beachhead exploits. Vulnerabilities get multiplied across larger exposed areas. Compromised credentials easily impact broader target scopes. Troubleshooting incidents prove exponentially more complex, tracing interconnectivity. Failure to properly implement and maintain network segmentation undermines core security capabilities. Continuous review avoids gaps from overlooked system relationships.

SOFTWARE-DEFINED SEGMENTATION

Network functions virtualization through software-defined networking abstracts physical topology for programmatic controls. It accelerates policy design, testing, enforcement, and change management. Segmentation rules dynamically provision pathways between workloads oblivious to physical constraints. Micro-segmentation virtualizes networks to isolate East-West host-host traffic embedded in switches. The policy defines which workloads interact based on attributes like application type versus assumptions of trust on individual hosts. SDN automation streamlines security incident response actions like quarantining compromised segments.

HYBRID CLOUD SEGMENTATION

Securing hybrid interconnectivity poses unique segmentation challenges. On-premise and cloud systems assume separate trust into a consistent security model. VPN or direct connectivity enables exchange while isolating resource types and preventing unintended access. For example, a database may connect to specific application servers yet remain invisible to others. API-driven security modules define and enforce micro-segmentation policy consistently across environments. SDN principles virtualize hybrid infrastructure into policy-defined, service-oriented topologies mitigating complex physical sprawl.

Securing Wireless Networks

WIRELESS NETWORKING GROWTH AND RISKS

As wireless connectivity grows ubiquitous, wireless networks have become a primary means of network access extending beyond traditional wired infrastructures. Their inherent properties also introduce risks requiring mitigation through considered security practices. Wireless networking advantages include flexibility, density, and reduced deployment costs compared to cabling. However, the broadcast transmission medium makes signals prone to sniffing if not properly secured. Additionally, a proliferation of personal smart devices expands potentially unmanaged avenues of access. Understanding threats specific to wireless aids hardening deployments against evolving attacks.

WIRELESS ENCRYPTION

Encryption scrambles wireless signals at the data link layer into unintelligible form without the proper cryptographic keys, safeguarding communications confidentiality and integrity. WPA/WPA2 Personal using pre-shared keys (PSK) provides consumer-grade protection if complex keys don't get publicly shared or brute-forced. WPA/WPA2 Enterprise employing 802.1X authentication with RADIUS servers introduces authentication for stronger access control to network segments. Both rely on the Advanced Encryption Standard (AES) symmetric cipher, though legacy protocols remain in use. Ensuring wireless networks employ the latest recommended encryption standards establishes a core baseline defense.

SSID BROADCASTING

Disabling SSID broadcasts in beacon frames prevents casual eavesdropping on network identifiers that could aid targeted attacks. However, this offers limited security through obscurity since SSIDs still get shared in association frames. Balancing visibility for usability versus unnecessary signaling requires consideration. Disabling SSIDs should supplement, not replace, encryption and other controls.

MAC ADDRESS FILTERING

MAC address filtering on wireless access points provides a basic access control allowing only specified device MAC addresses after authenticating identities. However, MAC addresses get spoofed relatively easily, limiting effectiveness as a primary control. The role lies in the rapid lockout of locally connected unknown devices rather than comprehensive access management.

ROGUE AP DETECTION

Unauthorized rogue access points pose security risks and performance issues on wireless networks if connected without inspection or integration. Wireless intrusion prevention systems (WIPS) detect, locate, and help remediate rogue infrastructure using network anomaly detection. They optimize wireless spectrum use across managed installations, avoiding interference and security gaps from rogues.

GUEST NETWORK ISOLATION

Guest networks provide open wireless access to visitors while isolating their traffic from internal infrastructure through VLAN segmentation, filtering, and firewall rules. This reduces the risk of exposing sensitive data from personal devices lacking security features. Best practices include applying usage quotas and expiring sessions after inactivity periods.

NETWORK PERIMETER SECURITY

Wireless extends network perimeters unpredictably, undermining traditional physical security assumptions. Intrusion prevention systems detect unauthorized nearby access points surveilling internal transmissions. Firewalls enable security zones to restrict wireless mobility throughout environments based on need and risk assessments. Micro-segmentation creates enclaves isolating IoT, BYOD, and guest systems from production assets. Wireless security additionally involves disaster recovery and business continuity considerations around maintaining the availability of mobility services supporting remote and teleworker access. Strategies address risks from events like natural disasters compromising wired infrastructure relied upon for wireless controller connectivity and management. Overall, defense-in-depth recognizes wireless as core attack surfaces, necessitating safeguards proportional to expanding dependencies and coverage footprints.

WIRELESS ACCESS CONTROLS

Access points act as primary control points integrating authentication, encryption, and micro-segmentation policy enforcement. Enterprise wireless LAN controllers (WLC) centrally configure and enforce standards across AP fleets to streamline management. Secure protocols for management channels prevent exploitation of administrative interfaces. User and device profiles grant tiered access privileges based on need and functions versus open availability. RADIUS or active directory federation services facilitate standardized access controls across organizational boundaries as wireless blend environments. Regular audits close gaps to evolving threats, exploiting potential misconfigurations.

SIGNAL HARDENING

Beyond encryption, techniques reduce exposure through physical signal hardening controls:

- Adjust power levels and antenna patterns to minimize propagate coverage precisely to intended areas, limiting scan ranges.

- Utilize spectrum analysis detecting interferers or rogues on overlapping channels causing performance or security issues.

- Incorporate materials blocking RF signals within shielded enclosures requiring credentials like elevators or conference rooms.

- Deploy wireless intrusion prevention systems to monitor airspace health and detect anomalies on the RF protocol levels outside typical IDS/IPS.

These physical practices supplement logical controls by reducing unnecessary signatures, benefiting attackers scanning for network identifiers.

CHAPTER 7
Network Monitoring and Threat Detection

Network Traffic Analysis

NETWORK TRAFFIC AND INFRASTRUCTURE VISIBILITY

Monitoring network traffic provides insights into operational health, user behaviors, and potential security issues. Deep visibility into packet flows, conversations, applications, users, and systems fosters an understanding of the constantly changing infrastructure supporting business services. Analytic techniques include sniffing traffic, inspecting contents, following streams, decoding protocols, applying baselines, and tracking anomalies. When combined with critical asset information and threat intel, traffic monitoring strengthens defenses, incident response, forensics, and compliance.

NETWORK TAPS AND SPANNING

Traffic inspection requires unobstructed access to live packet streams. Network TAPs provide passive mirrored ports for hardware and software probes without interfering with production traffic. Switches enable spanning or mirroring to copy specific VLAN or port traffic for analysis. Inline TAPs replicate streams to multiple tools simultaneously. Well-placed TAPs balance coverage needs by minimizing packet delays or loss of fidelity from complex topologies.

CAPTURING AND STORAGE

Network packet brokers distribute traffic to tools based on flexible forwarding rules. Capture appliances buffer streams at full line rate for application or protocol decoding requiring demanding throughputs. Storage systems retain flows for forensics, incidents, and compliance auditing requiring retrospective investigation. Minimizing storage overhead through filtering, compression, and tiered retention tempers costs while satisfying business needs.

DEEP PACKET INSPECTION

Beyond surface inspection of packet headers and payloads, deep analysis deconstructs transport and application layer protocols to discern intent within encrypted streams, becoming increasingly prevalent. Protocol decoding yields sessions, conversations, and semantics unavailable to surface inspections alone. This supports visibility into encrypted tunnels and the communications occurring within virtual private networks or HTTPS for a more complete understanding of activities and any deviations.

TRAFFIC DECRYPTION

Some tools decrypt captured traffic streams by intercepting and exporting keys or certificate information from endpoints using them. However, decryption remains legally and practically complex, risking interception of plaintext data without authorization. Careful controls avoid privacy and compliance implications by focusing on metadata and limiting storage durations without business justifications. Focused decryption assists penetration testing yet proves too processing intensive for production monitoring.

ANALYTICS TECHNIQUES

Traffic analysis leverages diverse techniques to discern meaning from packet flows:

Statistics - Volumes, bitrates, error flags, and usage trends offer visibility to optimize operations and plan growth.

Baselines - Normal behaviors establish expected parameters to detect anomalies or attacks.

Signatures - Known threats get detected through pattern matches focused on malicious signatures filtered from normal activities.

Machine Learning - Advanced algorithms discern relationships within high volumes of traffic, assisting hunting activities and predictive capabilities.

Protocol Analysis - Decoding application contents provides additional context compared to superficial headers alone.

Traffic Reconstruction - Piecing together bidirectional conversations yields insights from full context unavailable from isolated directions.

The right mix of statistical, behavioral, heuristic, and machine learning techniques filters insights from petabytes of network traffic for security teams.

TRAFFIC ANALYSIS TOOLS

Diverse commercial and open-source tools address various traffic monitoring and analytic needs:

- Network sniffers capture raw packets without inspection (Wireshark, tcpdump).
- NSM systems reconstruct sessions and filter known threats (Bro, Suricata).
- Probes decode protocols and flag anomalies (Zeek, NfSen).
- DPI tools inspect encrypted payloads with acceleration (RSA NetWitness, Darktrace).
- Analytics platforms apply ML to metadata (Cisco Stealthwatch, Anthropic).
- Network performance monitors troubleshoot issues (SolarWinds, Cisco NX).

Strategically combining toolsets supports the full analytic workflow from initial collection through inspection, hunting, and long-term investigation phases.

COMPLIANCE AND PRIVACY

Network surveillance requires responsible policies balancing security needs with compliance and privacy obligations. Approvals, access controls, metadata anonymization, and short retention periods minimize overcollection risk. Audit logs establish the chain of custody for investigations. Focusing analytic priorities on high-priority assets secures the most sensitive information first before expanding perimeter visibility.

Detecting Anomalies

ESTABLISHING BASELINES

Anomaly detection programs begin by establishing typical operational baselines. Sensors monitor critical systems, applications, users, and network segments, collecting vast metrics streams. Analytical platforms aggregate telemetry, filter noise, and derive statistical profiles quantifying normal behaviors across monitored entities. Repetitive patterns within volumes establish expected boundaries and distributions for individual indicators and their interdependencies. Periodic validation ensures profiles reflect organic changes to monitored entities not captured through initial snapshots alone.

BEHAVIORAL ANALYSIS

Statistical and machine learning techniques scrutinize flows, identifying irregularities compared to established benchmarks. Simple thresholds flag deviations from typical patterns like large file transfers. Regression and cluster analysis discern correlations exposing activities veering from common relationships. Entropy checks gauge unexpected protocol usages, information flows, or traffic localities. Principal component analysis reduces dimensionality to fundamental factors for detecting anomalies within high-cardinality environments. Neural networks discern subtle patterns within distributed systems that are difficult to encapsulate algorithmically. Process mining recreates workflows to pinpoint policy violations or control divergences.

EXTERNAL CONTEXT

Threat intelligence contextualizes anomalies, separating true positives requiring focus from minor fluctuations or inevitable statistical outliers. Blacklists expose known bad IPs, domains, or file hashes associated with past incidents. Sandboxing deduces malware behaviors, providing reference points. Dark web monitoring profiles threat actors and planned campaigns informing hunting. Geopolitical risk factors indicate the Likelihood of targeted attacks. Dark data archives preserve past anomalies for longitudinal intelligence gaining through retrospective discovery. Over time, threat profiles emerge, reducing 'unknown unknowns' to improve prioritization and automated detection.

INVESTIGATION AND TUNING

Analysts vet-flagged irregularities through correlation with contextual intelligence for remediation guidance. False alarms refine analytics by incorporating analyst feedback into updated normalcy profiles and detection logic. The research traces the root causes of real issues to strengthen controls. Incorporating outcomes closes loops, continually self-tuning models to optimize accuracy and efficiency as environments evolve beyond static baselines.

ANOMALY TYPES

Specific anomaly types provide lenses for monitoring objectives:

1. **Point Anomalies -** Identify statistically improbable individual data points.
2. **Contextual Anomalies -** Deviations considering contextual or relational attributes.
3. **Collective Anomalies -** Patterns across many related entities simultaneously.
4. **Internal Anomalies -** Deviations within singular metrics or entities over time.
5. **External Anomalies -** Deviations correlating with outside contextual factors.
6. **^Concept Drift -** Changes indicating underlying conditions shifting monitored populations.

Supervised learning leverages past known issues to bolster unsupervised anomaly detection resilience, detecting novel variants beyond rule-based definitions alone.

DETECTION CHALLENGES

Completeness remains elusive, considering the volume, variety, and velocity of monitoring sources. Concept drift invalidates static profiles requiring frequent tuning. Massively distributed and opaque systems challenge measurement and contextualization. Imbalanced and incomplete training data biases detection unfairly. Structural changes complicate direct comparisons over time. Sophisticated adversaries purposefully distort fingerprints to evade attribution. Continuous improvement counterbalances these factors through creative techniques addressing detection limitations strategically.

REGULATORY CONSIDERATIONS

Anomaly detection processing personal data necessitates compliance with regulations like GDPR and CCPA. Techniques minimize identification risks through anonymization, differential privacy, and short data retention, aligning with purpose limitations principles. Oversight ensures fairness to avoid marginalizing groups and provides redress for improperly flagged individuals. Strategic programs balance security objectives with privacy through responsible design and governance.

Responding to Network Incidents

INCIDENT RESPONSE PLANNING

Effective incident response begins with thorough preparation. Response plans document defined roles, procedures, contact lists, evidence-collection processes, review practices, and documentation requirements. Playbooks map workflow paths for common scenarios and escalation paths. Tabletop exercises test plans, evaluate gaps, and assess team coordination. Readiness reviews validate tools, access controls, and availability aligned with SLAs. External support agreements aid response scale during major events. Retaining legal counsel assists in compliance with regulatory obligations. Overall planning establishes the crucial capabilities, authorities, and team coordination, reducing chaos during real events.

INCIDENT DETECTION

Network-based monitoring serves as a primary detection avenue. Analytics flag abnormalities from logging platforms, IDS/IPS, flow tools, network taps, and change auditing. User reports and asset scans also reveal issues. Centralized security information and event management platforms correlate alerts for contextualized investigations. Incident trackers catalog full lifecycles from detection through resolution and review processes. Communities exchange intelligence for correlating internal findings alongside broader attacks.

INITIAL RESPONSE

Rapid triage indicates the criticality and resources required. First responders isolate compromised systems through firewalling or networking ACLs, limiting spread. They change credentials for impacted privileged accounts. Volatile memory acquisition preserves ephemeral evidence. Network traffic records, logs, and configuration snapshots document baseline states. Assets get disconnected from production to contained environments for further analysis without affecting availability or exposing other devices.

ON-SITE RESPONSE

Severe incidents warrant assembling on-site response teams. They leverage digital forensics tools directly accessing target systems, bypassing potential evidence manipulation by active adversaries. Physical verifications supplement remote investigations, establishing authoritative timelines. Responders notify regulatory bodies, and press teams coordinate communication strategies.

TACTICAL ANALYSIS

Methodically analyze indicators extracted from affected devices leveraging threat intelligence platforms. They corroborate any recognizable tools, techniques, or procedures. Sandboxing executes suspect files observing behaviors. Memory forensics parses volatile data. Network traffic reconstruction pieces together lateral movements and exfiltration attempts. Findings triage follow-on investigative steps toward root cause identification and remediation validation.

SHORT TERM REMEDIATION

Initial containment actions isolate compromised systems to prevent further propagation. Next, responders apply emergency patches, resolving known exploited vulnerabilities or blocking active backdoors. Forensic images capture affected devices for long-term analysis in contained labs. Investigations continue while production systems restore operations through rebuilding, reimaging, or changing credentials as indicated to isolate traces.

LONG TERM REMEDIATION

Deeper remediation hardens any weaknesses indicated by long-term forensic findings. Architectural changes segment attack surfaces. Policy updates address behaviors allowing compromise. Additional monitoring and controls detect indicators of compromise possibly remaining. Responders validate remediation effectiveness through penetration testing or continued monitoring.

POST INCIDENT ACTIVITIES

Lessons learned incorporate feedback and improve response plans, tools, skills, and controls. Regulators get notified as required. Public relations teams manage reputational impacts through controlled transparency. Privileged access gets reviewed for any abuse indicators. Auditors evaluate control lapses and test improved defenses. Metrics track timelines for continuous improvement programs. Ongoing threat hunting validates full removal of adversary presence or changes.

SHARING ECONOMY

Through legal frameworks, communities facilitate indicators and lessons learned, improving defenses industry-wide versus isolated responses benefiting singular bad actors. Standardized format exchanges anonymize sensitive details for privacy. Regulated sharing balanced security and cooperation amid regulations and liability.

CHAPTER 8
Advanced Network Security

Zero Trust Architecture

TRUST PARADIGM EVOLUTION

Traditional security models assume well-defined protected perimeter boundaries enabling trust within domains once authenticated at gates. However, mobility, cloud adoption, and hybrid work have dispersed once-isolated environments into interconnected ecosystems. Expanded networks complicate static controls as boundaries dissolve. Meanwhile, advanced breaches penetrate perimeter defenses, undermining trust assumptions upon which legacy approaches rely. This necessitates rethinking trust, fundamentally securing each resource interaction rather than entire network zones predominantly.

ZERO TRUST PRINCIPLES

Zero trust architecture principles reverse legacy inside/outside classifications, instituting strict, context-aware access controls without default open access internally or externally. It treats all requests - from any location, device, application, or user - as unverified until authentication, authorization, and policy enforcement transpire before approvals through security-first gates. Network position or existing sessions alone no longer imply inheritance privilege escalations demand continuous verification. Policies accommodate approved access profiles to resources on demand versus open-ended entitlements, presuming assets remain secured once authenticated initially anywhere on old perimeters.

MICROSEGMENTATION

Strict micro-segmentation emerges as a core zero-trust architectural practice realigning policy enforcement from network layers towards predetermined application and workload profiles. It inserts security-aware infrastructure throughout environments, dividing environments into countless minute segments isolated using layered controls, including network ACLs, firewalls, routers, load balancers, and Software-Defined Perimeter (SDP) technologies. These ensure only intended communication exchanges occur between authorized components following least privilege principles. Precision controls prohibit unintended integration points. Attackers could pivot laterally, compromising additional resources after initial infrastructure penetrations.

ACCESS CONTROLS

Central to zero trust, granular access controls govern each resource interaction at scale. Authentication must pass stringent multi-factor validation beyond usernames and passwords before authorization consideration. Policy codifies acceptable activities for specific users from certain locations, devices, or applications into finite verifiable profiles. Checks inquire about contextual attributes, entitlements, and resource attributes mitigating compromise risks from credential abuse since access persistence no longer exists even internally post-login. Detection reigns paramount monitoring for anomalies compared to expected, approved usage patterns. Automatic responses isolate unauthorized deviations immediately ahead of impacts.

PRIVACY AND USABILITY

While securing interactions, zero trust maintains user productivity through transparent single sign-on experiences. Federated identity management simplifies compliance with privacy obligations through selective attribute release limitations, only granting approved authorizations without full identity exposure. Management remains overhead practical through automated policy generation, delegation, and enforcement consistency relying on the standardized open interface. Continuous monitoring minimizes disruptions through intelligent, low-friction adaptive policies optimizing balance accessibility requirements.

TOOLS AND TECHNOLOGIES

Diverse tools execute zero-trust architectures:

- SDPs (Cisco ACI, AppGate) enforce micro-segmentation policies across hybrid IT.
- VPNs/ZTNA (Palo Alto, Zscaler) govern all remote access interactions.
- IAM (Okta, OneLogin) provides backend identity sources for access controls.
- FWaaS (CheckPoint, Fortinet) inserts perimeter-less micro-segmentation points.
- NAC (Aruba, Cisco) evaluates the health of endpoints before WiFi or wired approval.
- SIEM (Splunk, IBM QRadar) provides centralized monitoring for anomalies.

Strategically combining complementary platform capabilities addresses the principles across physical, virtual, and cloud infrastructure at massive scales, continuously verifying each transaction strictly as the optimal balance between access and security amid flexible operational needs.

ADOPTION CHALLENGES

While compelling, zero-trust adoption faces realities:

Technical Debt
Legacy systems lack integration points for modern policy schemes.

Organization Buy in
Cultural shifts require executive sponsorship and change management.

Skills Shortages
Expertise remains a nascent field requiring upskilling and coordination.

Immature Solutions
Tools require real-world maturation proven at the largest deployments.

Compliance Obligations
Regulations must align, permitting granular, automated processing.

Resource Investments
Significant funding supports purchase, integration, and operations.

Advanced Firewall Configurations

FIREWALL FUNDAMENTALS

Firewalls provide basic network protections by selectively permitting or denying transmission between zones. They filter traffic at layer three and above, examining packet headers and payloads and executing configured access control rules evaluating source, destination, protocols, ports, and other attributes before either allowing passage into protected resources or dropping connections. Stateful packet inspection tracks established flows dynamically, opening pinholes for responses strictly adhering to initiated conversations. Basic firewalls strengthen protections beyond open perimeter designs, but introducing advanced configurations elevates security stratifications.

PACKET FILTERING

Beyond permitting mere connections, advanced filtering scrutinizes malware indicators within application layer contents. Signatures identify known malicious patterns through pattern matching, while heuristics flag suspected payload anomalies. Protocol decoding supports context-aware filtering, dissecting application semantics hidden within encrypted streams. Stateful protocol analysis further restricts applications functioning according to expected transmission behaviors, enforcing normalization, and eliminating exfiltration avenues or evasion techniques masking true intents. Machine learning correlates traffic attributes, detecting stealthier threats leveraging model-driven risk assessments supplemented by traditional rulesets.

THREAT INTELLIGENCE

Interfacing firewalls with dynamically updated intelligence feeds automatically blocks known bad IP addresses, domains, and file hashes before harm materializes. Sandboxing capabilities execute code within contained environments, observing behaviors and detecting callbacks or anomalous activity warranting blocking through policy. Emulation exposes evasion techniques attempting to circumvent Detection evasion before approval of protected resources. Monitoring detects known CnC behaviors emerging through lateral movements correlating internal observations with external context, enriching understanding of potential compromise states requiring quarantines or remediations across connected infrastructures. Intelligence strengthens defenses against previously unseen threats indicated within adversary infrastructure itself through contextual blocking at network perimeter boundaries.

WEB APPLICATION FIREWALLS

Specialized WAF protection profiles apply specific filtering around web services, inspecting HTTP requests, identifying vulnerabilities, malware payloads, or policy violations passed URIs, headers, parameters, file uploads, SQL injections, and session hijacking behaviors. They enforce input sanitization, output encoding, and normalization, eliminating exploits entering through application layers. Advanced constructs apply heuristics to track anomalies, rate limiting, and bot detection, mitigating DDoS and account takeover attempts.

MICROSEGMENTATION

Advanced zones enforce fine-grained segmentation microservices using dynamic firewall capabilities. This subdivides environments into security domains around approved authorization entitlements applied service-to-service. Centralized management provisions policies automatically through templating as infrastructure scales, prohibiting unintended exposure across workloads according to least privilege principles. Rules leveraging group permissions and tunnel encryption further enforce application-aware enclaves resilient against lateral movements across components. Should breaches occur, segmentation limits spread localizing containment efforts according to zoning.

ORCHESTRATION

Central management planes simplify policy orchestration, handling security complexities of dynamic, distributed infrastructures through centralized application programming interfaces (APIs). Templates, automation, and role-based access controls standardize rule constructions across firewall estates while delegation accelerates deployments. Integration with other security functions closes loops through shared context, improving detections, blocking, and remediations coordinated between connected points, fortifying overall resiliency. Change management tracks policy alterations, maintains compliance and audit trails for investigations, and improves response capabilities between connected infrastructure layers, firewalls, and intelligence sources, enriching monitoring capabilities shown above static devices alone.

ARTIFICIAL INTELLIGENCE

Advanced firewall deployments leverage AI-enhancing capabilities through unsupervised machine-learning techniques. Anomaly detection profiles normal behaviors, flagging deviations across correlated security logs requiring investigation or preemptive isolation. Neural analysis of patterns generalizes protections, classifying potential threats indicated through outlier detection beyond known definitions alone. Cloud-based orchestration platforms provide scalable processing power that inspects vast volumes, velocities, and varieties, surpassing rule-based restrictions alone. Strategic curation and tuning ensure techniques optimize security demands according to contexts without over-enforcement risks impacting usability or compliance requirements.

Secure Cloud Networking

CLOUD NETWORKING BENEFITS

Leveraging elastic cloud networking capabilities streamlines operations through consolidated infrastructure, delivering improved agility, scalability, and cost optimizations compared to legacy on-premises environments. Cloud providers assume responsibilities for maintaining baseline physical and virtual networking, reducing overhead through standardized templates, automated provisioning, and pay-per-use pricing, and reducing upfront capital expenditures. IT teams self-service provision isolated, isolated subnets and VPN interconnects on-demand for rapid service delivery cycles. Distributed workforce accessibility gains rely on accessible public connectivity, while hybrid models merge cloud resources with existing data centers. Overall, flexibility and robust capabilities attract workloads leveraging cloud scale. However, security must evolve holistically, securing expanded surface areas and distributed ownership models accompanying these shifts.

NETWORK SEGMENTATION

Strict logical segmentation divides cloud infrastructure into isolated security domains enforcing micro-perimeters. Network ACLs, security groups, and edge firewalls filter approved communication between named instance groups modeling authorized application topologies according to least privilege principles. AWS VPCs, Azure VNets, and GCP VPCs establish isolated network boundary zones dividing sensitive components such as databases, application tiers, and public-facing services, preventing lateral movements. DNS namespaces further delineate services from one another, mitigating risks from unintended integrations. Regular reviews validate entitlements and prune stale permissions, elevating dynamically provisioned defenses proportionally with requirements.

NETWORK ACCESS

All infrastructure access transits through centralized ingress and egress points applying fine-grained filtering. Private endpoint gateways strictly govern administration plane access leveraging VM hosts, bastion hosts, and JIT enforcement. Public load balancers and application delivery controllers situated between instances and the internet, leveraging WAF, DDoS mitigation, and rate-limiting techniques. Private APIs standardize programmatic access controlling access policies through rate limits and authentication schemes. Remote access VPNs integrate multi-factor protections, establishing always-on VPN architectures to prevent exposure of management traffic. Centralized logging tracks CLI, console, and API activities, supplementing auditing and forensics and improving cloud security posture management.

CLOUD NETWORK SECURITY

A diverse set of controls executes layered protections:

- A cloud-delivered firewall as a service/NGFW (AWS Shield Advanced, Azure Firewall Premium) provides UTM capabilities.

- DDoS protection (Azure DDOS Protection, Cloudflare Warp) defends from volumetric attacks.

- Web Application Firewalls mitigate OWASP vulnerabilities (AWS WAF, Cloudflare Web Application Firewall).

- Network Access Controls evaluate endpoints security posture (Cisco CloudVision NAC).

- Serverless Network Functions (CheckPoint, Zscaler) govern ephemeral workload security.

- Cloud-native IPS (AWS GuardDuty, Azure Sentinel) detects anomalies across correlated logs.

- Cloud-integrated SIEMs (Splunk Cloud, IBM Resilient) provide centralized visibility.

- Zero Trust Network Access governs all infrastructure access (Cisco Duo, Cloudflare Zero Trust).

Strategic integration secures dynamic, distributed cloud networks leveraging provider and third-party capabilities through centralized management and automation at scale.

HYBRID INTEGRATION

Reliably connecting cloud resources back to existing environments necessitates hybrid networking protections. Site-to-site VPNs establish encrypted tunnels between on-premises and cloud networks governed by dynamic routing protocols. Direct Connect circuits provide dedicated private connectivity bypassing public routes. Virtual appliances inserted within hybrid WANs enforce consistent policies across all traffic governed by centralized orchestration into cloud-delivered security functions.

On-premises DMZ zones filter east-west traffic, integrating load-balanced VMs. Standardized security also extends to hybrid cloud platforms and container workloads deployed across public and private providers for consistent protection independently of the underlying infrastructure. Overall, hybrid designs consolidate visibility and strengthen connected perimeters between legacy and cloud-native services.

VISIBILITY AND ANALYTICS

Network and security analytics extract insights from log flows and vulnerability indicators, improving protections. Anomaly detection profiles traffic baselines are flagging deviations requiring investigation. Asset discovery census exposed running services and open ports across ephemeral and static resources, detecting configuration gaps. Vulnerability assessments scan configurations and codebases for misconfiguration weaknesses. Deception technologies harden attack surfaces, deceiving adversaries, assessing resilience, and improving response playbooks as attacks materialize, continuously correlating detections globally and strengthening overall network posture.

BOOK 3
Web and Application Security

CHAPTER 9
Web Security Principles

OWASP Top Ten

OWASP TOP TEN

The Open Web Application Security Project (OWASP) is a non-profit foundation devoted to web application security. Through their initiatives, such as the Top Ten Project and membership community, OWASP aims to help organizations develop, purchase, and maintain applications and APIs that can be trusted. One of their most impactful resources is the OWASP Top Ten, which provides a frequently updated ranked list of the most critical security risks associated with web applications. Understanding these top threats and prioritizing efforts to remediate them is a cornerstone approach for any entity looking to improve its security posture.

HISTORY AND METHODOLOGY

OWASP began publishing the Top 10 in 2003 based on its members' experiences with real-world vulnerabilities. The original list contained only injection flaws and broken authentication-related issues. Since then, it has evolved significantly based on emerging trends and new classes of attacks. To develop each new version, OWASP conducts worldwide surveys of security experts and analyzes vulnerability data from across the industry. They also review publicly reported vulnerabilities and security research materials. This data is then synthesized and organized into categories representing the top 10 most exploited flaws.

IMPACT OF THE TOP TEN

The OWASP Top 10 has become incredibly influential, with widespread adoption across both commercial and open-source communities. Many compliance frameworks and standards like PCI DSS explicitly reference it for application security requirements. Development teams consider the list during coding testing phases and when selecting security tools. Auditors also use it as a baseline checklist to scan for vulnerabilities. By focusing efforts to eliminate the top threats first, organizations can drastically reduce their overall risk profile. Most importantly, when issues higher on the Top 10 are patched, cybercriminals are forced to shift techniques, making the web more secure overall for all users.

CATEGORIES AND RISKS

The current 2023 Top 10 includes:

1. Injection - Code or queries can be injected and executed unintentionally by the application. This includes SQL, OS, and LDAP injection flaws.

2. Broken Authentication - Credentials are often not properly protected, allowing attackers to easily compromise legitimate users' accounts.

3. Sensitive Data Exposure - Applications frequently fail to protect sensitive data, including personal info, financial details, and authentication credentials.

4. XML External Entities (XXE) - XXE attacks abuse improperly configured XML parsers to expose internal files or retrieve external data to affect application execution.

5. Broken Access Control - Users are able to access unauthorized functions, view or modify other users' data, or access functionality outside their intended permissions level.

6. Security Misconfiguration - Keys, passwords, and sensitive files are often exposed due to server/application misconfigurations or default settings not being changed.

7. Cross-Site Scripting (XSS) - XSS flaws allow attackers to insert and run unauthorized scripts in a trusted, vulnerable website that are run in the security context of the current user.

8. Insecure Deserialization - Applications deserializing untrusted data can be manipulated to execute unintended or malicious commands.

9. Using Components with Known Vulnerabilities - When third-party components like libraries, frameworks, and other software modules have known security weaknesses but are still used - either without fixing the vulnerabilities or without accounting for their implications.

10. Insufficient Logging & Monitoring - Without proper logging and reviewing of logs, attacks may go unnoticed, and when noticed, incident response is challenging.

Each category is assigned a priority between P1-P3 based on the technical difficulty, potential business impact, and exploitability of attacks against that vulnerability category to help guide where projects and organizations should focus their efforts.

MITIGATION STRATEGIES

The Open Web Application Security Project provides specific guidance on mitigating each category of vulnerability:

For injection issues like SQLi, input validation, prepared statements, and output encoding are recommended. Broken authentication can be addressed via strong credential management, multi-factor authentication, password policies, and account security best practices. Encryption, access controls, and principles of least privilege can protect sensitive data and systems from exposure. XML security features, input filtering, and configuration supervision help tackle XXE and XSS flaws. Default credentials, settings, and unnecessary services should be removed to reduce the risk of misconfigurations.

TOOLS AND TECHNOLOGIES

To assist with following the OWASP Top 10 mitigations, there are various tools, technologies, and services available. Static application security testing (SAST) tools can scan code for vulnerabilities automatically during development. This includes open-source options like OWASP ZAP, commercial products from companies like

Veracode, and capabilities within integrated development environments (IDEs). Dynamic application security testing (DAST) crawls live applications to identify runtime issues. Web application firewalls (WAFs) provide real-time protection against exploits by filtering requests and responses according to rules. These rules can be configured based on the OWASP Top 10. Source code libraries like OWASP ESAPI and libraries specific to programming languages help implement common security functions securely. Penetration testing services can evaluate defenses through simulated attacks.

PRIORITIZING REMEDIATION

Even with tools and technology assistance, remediating all OWASP Top 10 issues simultaneously may not be feasible, depending on an organization's resources and risk tolerance levels. The OWASP Top 10 provides a useful prioritization guide, as not all categories have an equal business impact or technical complexity to fix. Higher-level risks like injection flaws, authentication vulnerabilities, and exposure of sensitive data generally merit attention before issues lower on the list, such as improper logging. For example, development teams could first focus on integrating input validation libraries and parameterizing queries (injection), rolling out multi-factor authentication (authentication), implementing automated scans with OWASP ZAP (all categories), and adding basic logging to key application functions.

ORGANIZATIONAL ALIGNMENT

Strong integration between security and development operations teams promotes effective OWASP Top 10 adherence. AppSec engineers can help embed security best practices into coding standards, conduct reviews, and manage tools. They remain involved throughout the release lifecycle. Development managers allocate time for security activities instead of treating them as an afterthought. Executive support ensures compliance is treated as a priority rather than an optional exercise. Support from legal/compliance teams ensures audit processes satisfy regulatory requirements, too. Security awareness programs promote a culture where vulnerabilities are detected and reported promptly. With organizational commitment and cross-functional cooperation, the OWASP Top 10 becomes a collaborative framework for holistic application security.

Secure Coding Practices

SECURE DEVELOPMENT LIFECYCLE

Building security into the development process from the start is crucial for producing applications that are robust and resilient over the long term. The secure software development lifecycle (S SDL) integrates security considerations at every phase - from initial planning and design through coding, testing, deployment, and operations. This helps avoid costly fixes downstream and prevents many common vulnerabilities. Like other best practices, an SSLC works best when supported by leadership and embedded into organizational culture through training programs and accountability measures.

PLANNING AND REQUIREMENTS

Beginning with clear requirements sets the stage for building the right security controls into applications. Threat modeling evaluates user roles and interactions to understand potential risks. Architecture reviews ensure that planned technical designs support necessary security functionality. Defensive coding standards promote techniques like input validation, output encoding, authentication, authorization, and session management from the ground up. Allocating time and resources to secure coding protects against the temptation to cut corners later in deadlines. Paying attention to security early avoids expensive repairs and better satisfies customer expectations.

SECURE CODING PRACTICES

Proper handling of untrusted data is paramount. All user input should be validated, formatted, and sanitized before processing to prevent injection attacks. When accepting filenames, paths, numbers, etc., check format and bounds. When outputting data, encode characters to avoid cross-site scripting risks in HTML, JavaScript, XML, etc. Authentication credentials must be stored securely, preferably using asynchronous hashing with "pepper" and salts. Authorization enforcement uses role-based access control to restrict functionality; the principle of least privilege limits data and actions based on the need to know. Defensive checks are applied consistently; don't assume clients operate as expected. Session management follows best practices for encryption, timeouts, and fixation prevention.

CONFIGURATION MANAGEMENT

Source control systems facilitate ongoing code reviews to identify concerns early. Tracking progress allows reverting code as needed. Infrastructure as code using tools like Terraform avoids surprise changes to deployed environments. Libraries and dependencies require due diligence vetting versions for vulnerabilities that may be transitively introduced. Configuration baselines covering servers, frameworks, and platforms defend against drift over time. SecureDevOps integration ensures security quality gates activities like testing and deployment. Automation reduces toil and enforcement variability.

CODE REVIEWS

Pair and peer programming catch mistakes as they happen. Standards-based review checklists focus on high-risk issues aligned with priorities like the OWASP Top Ten. Automated static and dynamic analysis tools detect common flaws at a scale that human reviews may miss. However, tools lack reasoning abilities, so human reviews bring insights into context and intent. Addressing flagged vulnerabilities improves quality and safety. With experience, organizations develop customized checklists and processes tailored to their technologies and risk environments.

TESTING

From the start, application tests validate requirements, and the actual behavior of codes matches design intentions. Unit testing verifies individual functions; integration testing validates how components interact as expected. Functional testing explores all use cases and boundary conditions, especially involving untrusted data. Remediating issues found during development improves robustness. Penetration testing then simulates real attacks to evaluate the effectiveness of defensive measures. Whether outsourced or in-house, pen tests provide an invaluable perspective on remaining risks and guidance. Fixing issues identified allows hardening for production use safely. Automated testing minimizes defects propagating unwittingly through developer workflows.

TRAINING AND TOOLS

Language-specific coding guidelines help developers code securely from the start. Frameworks offer features to assist with common security functions, avoiding errors from scratch construction. Integrated tools within IDEs can automatically check code syntax and logic. Static and dynamic analysis tools validate designs and detect vulnerabilities at speed and scale beyond human capabilities. But tools are not foolproof; nuanced issues may evade detection or generate too many unactionable alerts. Experienced security engineers provide guidance on the interpretation of results. On-going training programs instill best practices as standards evolve with emerging threats. Incentives like certifications recognize proficiency and motivation to progress skills. Overall, a learning environment promotes continuous improvement by all.

DEPLOYMENT AND OPERATIONS

Production rollouts require diligence to avoid regressions. Comprehensive testing validates all functionality in target environments, especially interactions between applications, services, and infrastructure. Hardening guides ensure servers and services do not expose unnecessary attack surfaces. Runtime protection tools like web application firewalls filter traffic vulnerabilities discovered post-deployment. Robust monitoring and logging enable the detection of anomalous behaviors or policy violations. Incident response plans coordinate activities to contain, eradicate, and recover from security events while minimizing impact. Coordinated vulnerability management practices and patch systems and deployed updates expeditiously based on risk. User engagement enhances defenses with controls to suit their needs and reports issues for remediation.

Web Application Firewalls

As web applications continue proliferating online services, the complexity of potential vulnerabilities grows concomitantly. While secure development practices attempt to "code securely," vulnerabilities may still be introduced. Web application firewalls (WAFs) provide an additional layer of defense at the network perimeter, protecting applications and the backend systems they interact with. By filtering and blocking suspicious patterns in HTTP traffic, WAFs help frustrate common SQL injections, cross-site scripting (XSS) attacks, file inclusion vulnerabilities, and more. They further complement secure development through continuous monitoring and rule-set adjustments.

INSPECTING HTTP REQUESTS AND RESPONSES

At a basic level, WAFs operate by examining all requests and responses passed to web servers. They leverage positive and negative security rules defined according to signatures of known exploits to flag anomalies. For requests, this means checking parameters, cookies, headers, and URI strings against rulesets. Responses are similarly scanned to prevent reflected XSS or sensitive data leakage. Beyond just signatures, some WAFs integrate machine learning to detect zero-day attacks or refine rules automatically over time based on traffic patterns and payloads. By inspecting traffic before it even reaches the web server, unwanted traffic can be blocked safely without crashing back-end services.

RULE CONFIGURATION AND MANAGEMENT

Security rules powering the WAF need thoughtful design and ongoing tuning. Rules stem from sources like the OWASP Top 10 to address common flaws but eventually gain customization based on specific applications protected. Negative rules outright block known bad IP addresses and request traits. Positive security rules whitelist expected good traffic parameters and formats. General rules act conservatively at first to avoid blocking legitimate users, with refinements relaxing protections gradually based on observed traffic patterns. Rule configuration interfaces range from simple GUI dashboards to command line tools, depending on capabilities. Some vendors offer pre-configured templates for instant rule-set imports. Mature rule management automates updating definitions for new Zero-Days autonomously.

DEPLOYMENTS AND PLACEMENTS

WAFs deploy in various forms - as hardware appliances residing inline, virtual appliances, or cloud-based services. Inline models intercept all requests before the website, whereas other models, like out-of-band, offer different connection models. Important architectural decisions consider capacity needs to handle expected traffic throughput without reducing performance. High-availability setups use active-passive or active-active cluster configurations for redundancy. Appropriate placements examine using WAFs at the origin web server itself versus load balancers and CDNs for better scalability with traffic volumes. Intranet applications may utilize WAFs at the network perimeter or DMZ zone for web servers. With experience, administrators evaluate the ideal balance of security, performance, and cost.

DETECTION AND PREVENTION TECHNIQUES

Various filtering techniques underlie WAF operations:
- Signature-based inspection - check payloads for patterns of known attacks
- Protocol validation - verify requests conform to HTTP specs

- Heuristic filtering - flag anomalous fields based on statistical analysis
- Context-sensitive escaping - encode output contexts properly
- URL/query normalization - sanitize parameter value
- XML parsing - validate XML bodies are well-formed
- Rate limiting - block excessive requests from a source
- Page request retries - alert on repeated fuzzing attempts
- Geo-blocking - blacklist regions with high botnets
- Malicious IP/domain blocking - prevent known bad actor sites

ADMINISTRATION AND MANAGEMENT

Robust administration capabilities within WAF platforms maximize effectiveness over time. Configuration interfaces resemble industry-standard management tools for firewalls, switches, and servers. Events, blocks, and allowed requests populate easy-to-navigate dashboards and reports. Logs stream to SIEM/log aggregators for deeper insights. Controls tune rule thresholds, exempt known good clients/IPs, update signatures automatically, or set blacklists/whitelists. Backups save configurations for disaster recovery. High-performance hardware or software appliances support real-time auditing of huge traffic volumes. Auto-scaling groups increase concurrency for bursting workloads. Health monitors minimize downtime from failures. System and security patches apply transparently.

CHAPTER 10
Securing Databases and Data

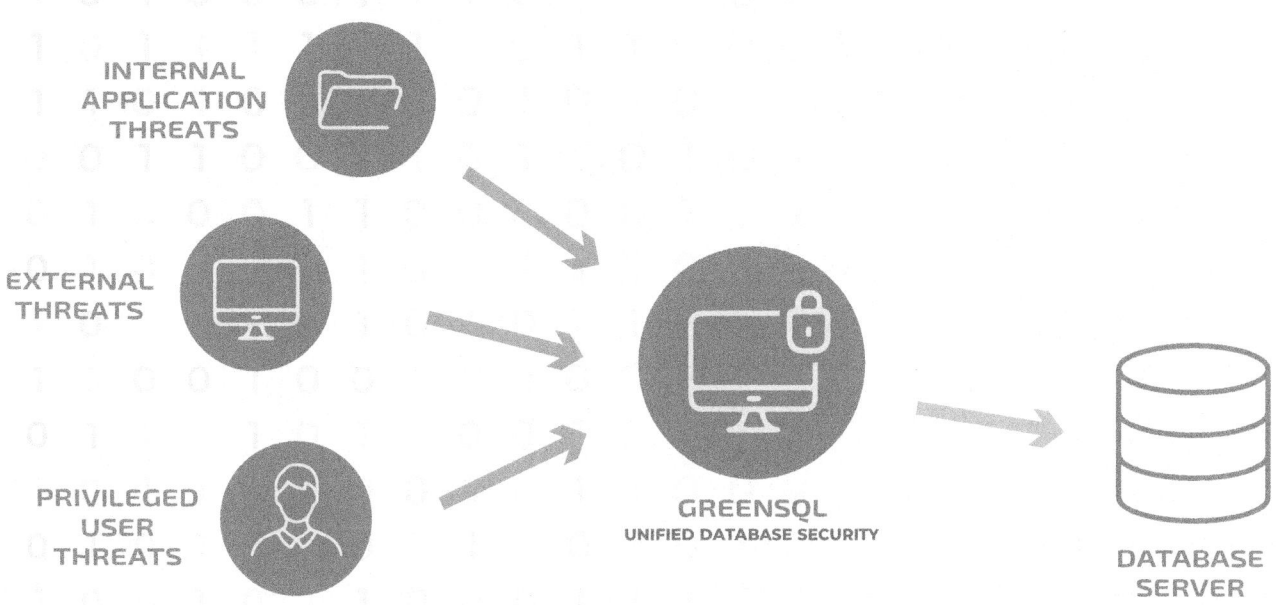

Database Security
INTRODUCTION TO DATABASE SECURITY

Regardless of scale or context, databases form the core persistence layer for applications and contain highly sensitive data worth defending. From small personal databases to sprawling multi-tenant cloud systems storing financial records, personal health information, intellectual property, and more - databases require robust protections to ensure the confidentiality, integrity, and availability of data assets. However, securing databases introduces unique challenges due to the technologies employed, the sensitive nature of contents, and distributed architectures involving applications, networks, and infrastructure. With care and diligence, practical controls hardened according to leading practices strengthen overall defenses.

PHYSICAL AND ENVIRONMENTAL SECURITY

For on-premise databases, physical access controls restrict premises entrance to authorized personnel. Server rooms subject equipment to environmental controls for cooling, humidity, and electrical safeguards. Disaster recovery sites geographically house infrastructure copies safe from local threats. Remote or cloud deployments rely instead on providers' security assurances across data centers like CCTV monitoring, badge access logging, and biometrics. Physical destruction or theft remains out of direct control. Overall, hardware/network perimeter defenses comprise the first line of layered protection.

NETWORK SEGREGATION AND ENCRYPTION

segregating database networks from less-trusted zones prevents attacks targeting adjacent systems. Firewalls, security groups, and routing policies confine approved communication paths. TLS-encrypted connections between applications and databases guarantee data integrity and confidentiality transit. Internal segmentation isolates read/write roles and sensitive databases. VPNs authenticate remote administrative access securely. Intrusion prevention systems inspect traffic for exploits before reaching systems. Regular audits ensure compliance with isolation and encryption standards.

IDENTITY AND ACCESS MANAGEMENT

Granular access controls configure minimum necessary privileges according to job roles using concepts like role-based access control (RBAC). Complex credentials and multi-factor authentication strengthen administrative logins exponentially. Monitoring detects anomalies like concurrent sessions and alerts teams. Just-in-time access removal for terminated employees avoids misuse. Centralized directory services synchronize credentials management. Self-service password resets balance security with convenience. Sensitive activities require approval workflows to mitigate risks and enable checks. Simplified yet secure permissions benefit both security and user experience.

CONFIGURATION HARDENING

Database builds follow templates, applying patches, avoiding unnecessary services, and removing default credentials to minimize the exposed attack surface. Parameterized queries mitigate injection risks. Audit logs securely track database schema and file changes. Encrypted backups prevent data loss from outages or malicious integrity incidents. Query performance optimization avoids computationally expensive actions like regular expressions. Host and container OS defenses fend off malware distribution and privilege escalation attempts targeting underlying infrastructure before reaching the database itself. Standard baselines withstand scrutiny and keep infrastructure updated.

MONITORING AND LOGGING

Comprehensive logging captures security-relevant database events, queries, access attempts, and policy violations to facilitate real-time monitoring and post-incident investigations. Automated alerts notify anomalies like unrecognized IP blocks suddenly initiating connections or repeated failed password attempts targeting administrator accounts. Log aggregation platforms correlate activities across systems to detect stealthy multi-stage attacks spanning applications and infrastructure. Logs are securely archived according to retention schedules and remain discoverable during litigation processes. Log inspection keys onto suspicious behaviors early using analytics like statistical outliers, unique identifiers, or keyword searches.

VULNERABILITY MANAGEMENT

Actively remediating known software defects prevents exploits from compromising data availability, integrity, or confidentiality. Coordinating vulnerability disclosure between DBMS vendors and client teams ensures patches promptly address critical issues. Scans validating installation of patches supplement configuration management testing configurations against benchmarks. Patching minimizes exposure during disclosure windows by leveraging zero-day subscriptions. Where patching introduces regression risks, compensating controls like network isolation contain threats until upgrades feasibly occur. Proactivity short-circuits attacks relying on publicly disclosed vulnerabilities.

API AND WEB APPLICATION SECURITY

For databases exposed via APIs or driven by frontends like PHP/ASP.NET applications, additional layered defenses apply. Input validation sanitizes payloads for queries and stored procedures. Least privilege principles curb database accounts' access from applications. Parameterized queries thwart injection regardless of invocation. Response encoding forestalls client-side injection risks. Authentication, authorization, and CORS policies regulate cross-domain access. Runtime application self-protection tools inspect API calls for policy violations. Web application firewalls filter requests and responses for anomalies according to rules. Defenses align holistically across tiers.

IDENTITY AND ACCESS MANAGEMENT CONSIDERATIONS

Ensuring appropriate access controls surround database assets requires attention to subtle nuances:

Schemas underlie relational databases' logical structuring of objects, data types, and table relationships. Privileges grant permissions over schemas, tables, views, stored procedures, and other components rather than directly accessing underlying operating system objects. Database roles consolidate underlying system users, reducing complexity. Membership rules activate role-based functionality based on authentication sources. Linked server definitions control cross-instance access between database instances. Certificates and asymmetric keys enable encrypting sensitive values like passwords during transit. Row-level security filters rows according to business logic and users' attributes. Dynamic management objects configure triggers and extended properties rather than altering base structures directly.

AUDIT AND COMPLIANCE ASSURANCE

Regulatory pressures surface to address breaches, privacy regimes, and contractual responsibilities through comprehensive auditing of database controls and activities:

Audit logs record security-relevant events, configuration changes, workflow approvals, queries, and account authentications efficiently stored off-host in a tamper-proof repository. Automated parsing tools investigate anomalies according to risk-based thresholds customized by domain expertise. Read-only snapshots isolate investigative copies to prevent interfering with production workloads. Vulnerability scans validate configurations to align with secure baselines, and patching routines address disclosed flaws promptly according to severity. Penetration testing ethically attempts to exploit environments to identify remaining weaknesses.

THIRD-PARTY RISK MANAGEMENT

Database-as-a-service (DBaaS) offerings, add-ons, backups, and other external integrations undermine security if not vetted and authorized carefully:

Vulnerability disclosure policies consider response timeliness and transparency expected for components outside administrative domains. Due diligence compares offerings comprehensively across privacy, security, support, and contractual terms before committing implementations or sensitive data. Sandbox deployments evaluate integration impacts before production authorization. Access controls specifically list permitted third parties and their privileges according to justified business needs. Logging tracks interaction details between first and third-party systems. Contract negotiations incorporate service-level agreements around areas like data confidentiality, integrity, availability, incident response, and auditing assurances. Overall, third-party risks require diligence proportionate to the sensitivity entrusted to external entities.

Data Encryption

IMPORTANCE OF DATA ENCRYPTION

As technology moves data storage and processing into cloud-based environments, encryption serves a vital role in securing sensitive information wherever it may travel or reside. Encryption scrambles plain text into ciphertexts that appear as unintelligible random sequences, protecting confidentiality even if intercepted or exposed unintentionally. Whether data rests on end-user devices, in transit over networks, or within corporate or cloud infrastructure - encryption establishes trust by safeguarding privacy and preventing unauthorized access or modification according to calculated cryptographic formulas. With the ever-increasing value of data assets and rising litigation risks from breaches, encryption elevates security and compliance postures for all organizations.

ENCRYPTION ALGORITHMS

Effective encryption relies on published, peer-reviewed algorithms proven cryptographically sound. Common symmetric algorithms like AES encrypt very efficiently using a shared secret key between parties. Public-key encryption leverages key pairs for easier key distribution with algorithms like RSA or Elliptic Curve. Hashing applies one-way functions deriving fixed-size representations of variable inputs with no decryption mechanism - used heavily for password storage and verifying data integrity. Older algorithms risk exploitation due to computing advances rendering keys guessable, so migrating periodically maintains protections. Algorithm selection considers strengths, weaknesses, and compatibility with protocols and standards within specific use cases.

KEY MANAGEMENT

Cryptographic keys form the bedrock of encryption systems. Strong key generation using cryptographically secure random number generators strengthens keys, resisting brute force guessing or backdoor access. Key sizes align with algorithm lifecycles, staying ahead of quantum computing threats when practicable. Split-knowledge controls distribute keys logically or physically between online and offline storage, reducing single points of failure. Rotation policies refreshing keys periodically or triggered by environmental changes increase resilience from compromise over time. Central key management systems enforce policies, log access for auditing, and automate provisioning, revocation, and backup workflows seamlessly.]

IMPLEMENTATION CONSIDERATIONS

Prudent encryption execution addresses challenges around performance, compatibility, availability, consent, and regulatory concerns:

- Hardware acceleration offloads computation overhead from general CPUs
- Format-preserving encryption maintains underlying data structures
- Application programming interfaces normalize interactions across platforms
- Transparent encryption streams unnoticeable to users and applications
- Centralized key stores deploy encryption once, unlocking everywhere
- Data labeling catalogs identifiers for protected, sensitive fields
- Access controls integrate encryption usage into authorization workflows
- Distributed key derivation scales management across decentralization
- Auditing logs demonstrate encryption fulfills contractual and legal duties
- Backups and disaster recovery coordinate encryption at rest and in transit
- Standards compliance like FIPS 140-2 achieves certifications for sectors

Deliberate engineering tackles realities to maximize usability alongside strong protections in realistic operational environments.

Data Backup and Recovery

WHY BACKUP AND RECOVERY MATTERS

Preserving availability through robust data protection represents a core security function. Whether due to natural disasters, errors, attacks, or hardware faults -

backups provide the ability to restore recent and historical data states. Backups help minimize losses from corrupted storage, files becoming unintentionally deleted or modified, ransomware encryption, and many other incidents disrupting production systems. By duplicating critical business data under secure management, backups safeguard intellectual property, enable continuity during maintenance, and facilitate forensic investigations into compromises. With the right strategy, backups significantly enhance overall resilience against unexpected events threatening operations or profitability.

DEFINING RECOVERY OBJECTIVES

Planning starts by classifying data sensitivities and legally mandated retention periods. Recovery time objectives (RTO) and recovery point objectives (RPO) capture service level expectations around maximum tolerated downtime and potential data loss, respectively, according to varying workloads and regulatory obligations. Understanding service disruptions' consequences quantifies risks informing protection needs: can hours of downtime be accepted, or are minutes required? Is losing the past day of changes tolerable, or must recovery occur from the last few minutes? Backup strategies optimize cost versus recovery capabilities based on objectives.

BACKUP METHODOLOGIES

Full backups capture entire datasets, establishing a restored baseline. Incremental backups since the last full or incremental saves storage tracking only changed blocks for efficiency. Differential backups retain all changes since the last full-encompassing increments missed potentially between restore points. Versioning retains history, avoiding overwriting for point-in-time recovery precision. Ideal schedules balance size, frequency, and window lengths according to Recovery Time Objectives (RTOs). Testing validates configurations work as designed. Storage targets require capacities that fit volumes while securely maintaining performance, durability, and offsite portability.

ON-PREMISE BACKUP

Dedicated backup servers locally attached via LAN rapidly protect critical systems, minimizing RTOs. Replication extends copies to additional local drives, dispersing risks. Nearline storage pools augment capacities economically tape or disk. Offsite vaulting ships' daily backups to secure foreign facilities, avoiding single points of failure. Backup software orchestrates policies consistently across operating systems and applications. Agents require no production disturbances embedding availability into policies. Rotation and retention standards comply with regulations.

CLOUD BACKUP

Service provider storage virtualizes assets scalably, accessing public clouds via high-speed links. Burst buffer capacities absorb peak demands without CAPEX. Geographically distributed regions replicate for data resilience, attaining 99.999999999% durability. Native standard or customized retention reduces egressing costs. Thin provisioning and variable-length deduplication optimize space. Auditing substantiates controls and service levels contractual SLAs reimburse outages. Hybrid strategies combine clouds with on-prem components, optimizing costs within tolerable RTOs/RPOs.

BACKUP MONITORING

Comprehensive oversight ensures continuous data protection functioning seamlessly. Agents check backups, verifying integrity against corruption or tampering. Logs record process status, failures, and remediations for forensic review. Alerts notify anomalies requiring immediate attention, preventing accumulations of technical debt. Auditing validates policy adherence across all infrastructure layers and is compliant with regulations. Periodic testing directly restores sample datasets within established windows, measuring realities against goals. Forensic abilities recover accidentally overwritten objects from secure air-gapped repositories when needed most critically.

RECOVERY FUNDAMENTALS

Orchestrated plans outline steps reproducible under stress. Documented roles clarify responsibilities for resource allocation and decision-making rapidly. Standard operating procedures automate the majority of workflows, reducing human errors and coordinating interdependent components. Isolation protects production stability, while side-by-side validation of restored backups validates resiliency against recurrence. Version tracking backtracks incremental states across application, OS, data, and configuration rollbacks granularly. Recovery rehearsals validate competencies annually against evolving risks. Redundant infrastructure increases confidence, absorbing demand spikes without disruption.

CHAPTER 11
Securing Mobile and IoT Devices

Mobile Device Management

As personal and corporate mobile device usage proliferates, IT security challenges evolve regarding confidentiality, integrity, and availability of data on these increasingly powerful platforms. Mobile Device Management (MDM) enables the central administration of fleets of smartphones, tablets, and other portable devices utilized both within and outside the workplace. With the right MDM solution configured according to best practices, administrators gain visibility over endpoints coupled with robust policy enforcement, securing proprietary information wherever accessed and strengthening compliance postures overall.

ENROLLMENT AND AUTHENTICATION

Onboarding commences by enrolling devices into MDM portals via specialized EMM agents installed onto devices. Initial configuration profiles deploy securing configurations, certificates, and credentials provisioned during staging. Multi-factor authentication applications augment access controls over sensitive resources. Remote wiping and passcode enforcement protect lost/stolen assets proactively. Unique identifiers correlate device, user, and network information assisting investigations. Enrollment generates an inventory establishing a trusted rooted configuration validated during runtime.

INVENTORY & COMPLIANCE

Configuration management catalogs hardware/software specifications, patches, and applications continuously. Operational dashboard visibility alerts requiring attention surfaced. Real-time remote actions like lock wipe optimize the response, minimizing risks and costs. Geofencing geolocations alert anomalies while enforcing jurisdictions. Jailbreak detection suspends unsupported devices until repaired by helpdesks. Compliance policies automate remediating violations, preventing accumulations. Reports substantiate attestation addressing audits productively.

APPLICATION MANAGEMENT

App storefronts provision pre-approved enterprise applications through centralized distribution, bypassing unauthorized title availability. Whitelisting constrains installation sources securely. Containerization segments personal and managed data logically per needs. Updates automate patching vulnerabilities without disruptions. Controls restrict background data/network usage according to mandatory locks. Runtime monitoring flags anomalies for revocation or further investigation as needed.

SECURITY & ENCRYPTION

Passcodes enforce alphanumeric complexities consistently. Biometric authentication strengthens verifications of multi-factor where available. Full-disk encryption protects stored data encrypted, preventing exposures. Remote wipe deletes all stored enterprise information immediately if missing, stolen, or non-compliant according to roles. IPsec/SSL VPN integrates devices into protected domains seamlessly. Traffic filtering ensures that only approved network resources are available. Permissions management constrains sensitive API vulnerability avoidance.

HELP DESK SUPPORT

Self-service troubleshooting guides resolve common issues expediently. Ticketing systems track support requests end-to-end centrally. Remote support capabilities diagnose connections collaboratively. Customizable COOP templates standardize communications streamlining. Lockscreen messaging alerts anomalies requiring attention, guiding users productively. Knowledge bases retain resolutions addressing recurring issues consistently. Surveys gather satisfaction, improving support quality proactively.

ANALYTICS & REPORTING

Usage reports identify patterns informing deployment refinement. Application analytics detect compromises warranting revocation rapidly. Location insights optimize coverage planning. Device health reporting alerts requiring replacement extending lifecycles. Customizable dashboard widgets consolidate actionable metrics. Log management retains forensic evidence for complaint investigations. Automation acts on anomalies, proactively sustaining protection levels of dynamic fleets.

IoT Security Challenges

THE EMERGENCE OF IOT

The Internet of Things (IoT) drastically expands the scope of interconnected devices beyond traditional computing platforms. Everyday objects gaining network connectivity and sensors deliver new conveniences yet introduce complex security challenges due to fragmented ecosystems, embedded designs optimizing simplicity over protections, and unprecedented scale. As an estimated 50 billion "things" connect globally by 2030, robust defenses require proactively addressing inherent IoT risks across product development life cycles.

DEVICE HETEROGENEITY

Unlike general-purpose computers, IoT incorporates diverse hardware across industries, lacking uniformity. From household appliances and wearables to industrial equipment and infrastructure components - each specialized class introduces varied processor architectures, memory constraints, and operating environments, complicating protections tailored appropriately. Legacy constraints challenge updating vulnerable devices post-deployment, enduring up to decades unattended. Such heterogeneity inhibits consolidated security solutions, necessitating customized approaches.

RESOURCE LIMITATIONS

Microcontrollers powering many IoT endpoints contain minimal memory, processor power, and battery life in balance. Rigorous protocols, patch routines, and endpoint hardening practices stress such limitations. Constrained environments necessitate lightweight protections, avoiding processing or storage overhead degrading usability. Constrained networks also affect inspection capabilities. Ingenuity optimizes core security features within bounds differing from conventional standards.

INSECURE DEFAULTS

Devices shipping with default credentials for ease of use introduce attack vectors if unaltered by naïve users as intended. Credential changes require significant developer workarounds that are not guaranteed to be user-invoked. Hardcoded backdoors persist in some secrets despite the availability of basic fixes. Lack of physical access hinders remediating vulnerabilities. Ensuring secure initial states demands transparency and cooperation across communities.

FRAGMENTED DEVELOPMENT

IoT emerges at the grassroots level, involving collaboration between varied specialties siloed previously - from chip designers to network engineers integrating specialized components lacking cohesion. The absence of centralized, prescriptive authorities spawns diverging practices slower coalescing under formalized guidelines. Shared vulnerability databases and common patch schedules similarly progress gradually, unifying historically incoherent fields.

OPERATIONAL CHALLENGES

Distributed management introduces scalability concerns by configuring billions of endpoints heterogeneously in unpredictable environments. Constrained connectivity frustrates patching post-deployment when feasible. Limited interfaces hinder comprehensive remote monitoring and troubleshooting. Updating firmware and software requires care, considering peripheral compatibility and avoiding inadvertent bricking. Unmanaged third-party services pose risks compounding with component lifetimes exceeding support lifespans. Overall operational maturity progresses sector by sector, gradually addressing realities.

Best Practices for Mobile and IoT Security

Pervasive mobile devices and Internet of Things infrastructures deliver efficiency yet expand attack surfaces, necessitating diligent defenses. While constraints complicate protections relative to general computing, established practices adapted appropriately strengthen postures cost-effectively when integrated systematically. This overview surveys fundamental techniques for minimizing vulnerabilities across domains through controls, detection capabilities, and responsive capabilities. Consistent execution as part of holistic strategies sustains assurances for users, organizations, and systems in the long term.

ACCESS CONTROLS

Robust access forms the base level, segregating authorized from unauthorized access. Configuring unique credentials complex and periodically refreshed raises guessing difficulty. Multi-factor authentication further strengthens verification for high-risk interfaces. Authorization controls grant the least privileged access according to roles. Revoking defunct credentials eliminates exposure windows promptly. Monitoring detects anomalous logins while alerting enables rapid response. Secure proxies also offload and inspect authentication for added resilience.

CONFIGURATION SECURITY

Consistent configurations underpin reliable operation. Standard templates deployed through centralized consoles establish security hygiene efficiently at scale rather than relying on end users. Encrypting sensitive data fields preserves confidentiality. Disabling unneeded services reduces vulnerabilities. Mandating secure protocols avoids downgrading connections. Keeping software updated via scheduled scans and rollouts patches vulnerabilities. Separating personal and corporate interfaces establishes appropriate boundaries.

APPLICATION CONTROLS

Orchestrated application deployment streamlines management. Pre-approving titles from managed stores reduces risk unpredictability. Restricting entitlement access avoids function hijacking. Signing installers ensures integrity. Silently updating in the background maintains efficacy without disruption. Monitoring runtime behavior profiles normal functionality, raising alerts on deviations. Integrated mobile threat defense capabilities also detect actively exploited vulnerabilities or unusual data exfiltration. Granular approval workflows on installs and access maintain agility.

ANOMALY DETECTION

Real-time context awareness fortifies defenses. Establishing user and device baselines enables the detection of abnormal locations, behaviors, or file accesses, indicating potential compromise. Centralized security platforms normalize and correlate alerts across multilayered protections for clarity. Machine learning algorithms further classify and prioritize anomalies according to modeled risks, reducing noise to focus resources. Geo-tracking also enables responsive actions like remote wiping when devices stray from approved regions. Proactive rather than reactive detection and investigation minimize exposure windows.

INCIDENT RESPONSE

Well-rehearsed response capabilities actualize protection promises. Automated playbooks enable consistent addressing of indications before escalating manually. Remote access facilitates swift on-device forensic investigation and remediation to contain the spread. Isolation capabilities suspend access while preserving evidence for review. Preservation and auditing maintain oversight during and after incidents for learning. Training staff strengthens expertise over diverse systems. Tabletop exercises validate runbooks under pressure. Effective response sustains assurances, whereas neglected post-compromise capabilities undermine deterrence.

CHAPTER 12
Cloud Security

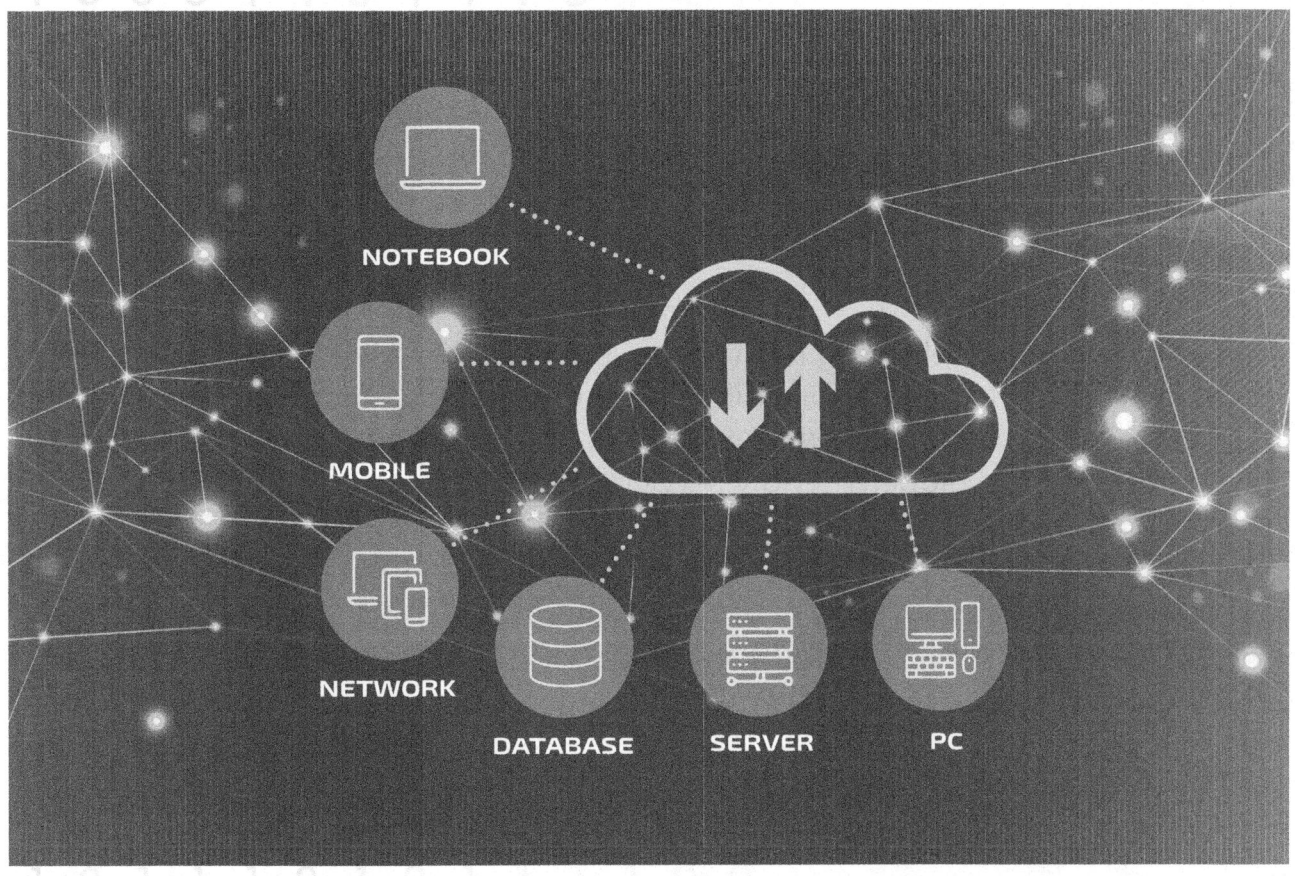

Cloud Service Models
CLOUD COMPUTING

Cloud computing delivers on-demand network access to scalable and configurable computing resources through virtualization technologies. This shared utility model optimizes costs through elastic allocation, bypassing inefficiencies of legacy physical infrastructure deployments. Major offerings include Infrastructure as a Service (IaaS), Platform as a Service (PaaS), and Software as a Service (SaaS). Each service model targets different layers representing increasing levels of abstraction and managed services from providers. Understanding core differences informs best aligning needs across rapidly evolving offerings.

INFRASTRUCTURE AS A SERVICE

IaaS delivers fundamental computing resources provisioned dynamically as virtual machines, virtual private servers, block or object storage, load balancers, and networks. Tenants access via programmatic interfaces administrating instances directly, while cloud providers handle physical infrastructure and hypervisors transparently. IaaS remains flexible, retaining full control over runtime environments suitable for large-scale deployments or migration scenarios. Costs scale with actual consumption, reducing waste. Major IaaS providers include Amazon Web Services, Microsoft Azure, and Google Cloud.

PLATFORM AS A SERVICE

PaaS extends IaaS, delivering managed platforms and abstracting infrastructure complexities. Users build applications atop integrated software stacks, including operating systems, databases, web servers, and programming languages/libraries bundled as developer-friendly services. Providers handle all hosting environment maintenance, patching, and scalability. Tenant focus shifts to rapid application development without internal administration. Heroku, Microsoft Azure App Service, and Google App Engine are popular PaaS platforms. This model improves portability across infrastructures, accelerating deployment.

SOFTWARE AS A SERVICE

SaaS encapsulates complete software solutions delivered as centralized web-based services. Users interact solely through unified client interfaces, avoiding installation, patches, or scaling. Providers retain all management responsibilities, while customers worry only about user-facing content customization. Examples include Dropbox, G Suite, Salesforce, and Workday, bringing flexible licensing to non-technical audiences. This full outsourcing model optimizes costs more than tactical outsourcing of hardware alone.

CHOOSING MODELS

IaaS retains maximal tenant control, prioritizing flexibility for large operations teams. PaaS accelerates app development through integrated tools masking infrastructure. SaaS automates maintenance best for software, replacing CAPEX with predictable OPEX. Hybrid models emerge, blending to split burdens strategically.

Due diligence considers advantages, limitations, lock-ins, and suitable use cases to meet actual needs long-term within budgets. As technology layers fuse across boundaries, ambiguity remains, though the underlying principles endure aligning clouds' shared resources optimally behind each environment.

PRICING STRUCTURES

IaaS/PaaS commonly charge hourly for instances and monthly for reserved/committed usage, avoiding unpredictable spikes. Costs align usage profiles, optimizing budgets while incentivizing efficient scaling. SaaS subscriptions focus on simple flat per-user pricing over fluctuating consumption, amenable to budgeting. Discounts emerge through long-term/bulk commitments or integrating multiple product lines together. Transparency ensures pricing matches actual business cases sustainably. Metrics, budgeting tools, and rightsizing monitor effectiveness while avoiding vendor lock-ins. With care, clouds responsibly optimize agility and resilience as services.

Shared Responsibility Model

As businesses increasingly leverage cloud infrastructures managed remotely by third parties, clarity surrounds accountabilities for security controls through a shared responsibility model. Responsibilities partition logically according to providers' and tenants' ability to independently manage particular aspects of the service. This division informs duties to uphold trust collaboratively despite physical/logical separations inherent in cloud architectures. Understanding each party's role strengthens overall assurance through cooperative execution.

DATA IN THE CLOUD

Tenants retain ownership and full control over customer data stored or processed utilizing provider services. Responsibilities include data classification, access controls, encryption, integrity checks, acceptable use identification, and retention/destruction policies in accordance with privacy and compliance requirements. Providers supply capabilities securing the environments within which customer data resides, though customers directly safeguard data itself and interfaces. Coordination clarifies assumptions and obligations, ensuring protection duties remain unambiguous regardless of infrastructure roles.

SHARED INFRASTRUCTURE SECURITY

Providers assume physical and environmental security covering data centers housing servers, storage, networking equipment, and cabling. This includes perimeter protection, intrusion prevention, video monitoring, redundancy, HVAC oversight, and equipment maintenance/replacement. Tenants administer logical access security encompassing user management, credentials, authorization, and authentication mechanisms. Cooperation establishes mutual trust where physical and digital responsibilities intersect holistically.

PLATFORM AND APPLICATIONS

Providers deliver infrastructure and virtualization, allowing customers to provision and configure operating systems, middleware, runtimes, databases, and applications. The tenant retains all duties over application security activities, including patching, configuration hardening, input validation, access controls, exception handling, and software/code quality. Cloud partners supply auditing and monitoring capabilities for tenants to observe their application behaviors for anomalies but leave interpretation and response duties to customers owning applications.

NETWORK AND PERIMETER SECURITY

Cloud operators isolate customer workloads within dedicated network segments, configure firewalls, network access control measures, and intrusion detection to protect the network perimeter while safeguarding against misuse of shared network infrastructure. Tenants independently defend application traffic flowing through provider networks by encrypting communications, implementing web application firewalls, and guarding exposed endpoints against attacks. Together, protections secure interconnectivity atop shared resources.

INCIDENT RESPONSE

Providers notify customers immediately upon identifying infrastructure breaches or vulnerabilities and coordinate remediation plans with tenants to contain impacts. Tenants directly address application layer intrusions through forensic analysis, patching, and recovery. Open communication enables containments encompassing responsibilities jointly, though action responsibilities remain clear according to data/application/infrastructure divisions.

Cloud Security Best Practices

Leveraging cloud services multiplies efficiency, though it also expands attack surfaces, requiring diligent security execution throughout deployment life cycles. Strategic best practices maximize protections by aligning people, processes, and technologies per shared responsibility models. Comprehensive yet practical techniques built upon core principles sustain assurances commensurate with risks when integrated according to contexts. This overview surveys fundamental approaches to bolstering cloud deployments responsibly.

ACCESS MANAGEMENT

Robust access controls establish a foundation segregating authorized from unauthorized identities and machines. Unique, complex credentials enforced via multifactor authentication strengthen verification. Just-in-time access and least privilege principles grant privileges narrowly according to approved roles. Monitoring anomalous behaviors promptly alerts anomalies, while automated response playbooks contain impacts. Access reviews validate de-provisioning and promptly revoke resigned accounts. Secure tokens assume machine identities safely. Overall, access management fortifies perimeters and availability.

NETWORK SECURITY

Network segmentation isolates workloads logically, addressing lateral movement risks through micro-segmentation. Firewalls filter approved protocols and sources/destinations defending exposed surfaces. Virtual private clouds and encryption-in-transit establish trusted tunnels between on-premise and cloud systems. Intrusion detection prohibits reconnaissance, while denial-of-service mitigations absorb volumetric assaults. Edge protections manage interconnectivity amid heterogeneous clients/applications. Network forensic abilities aid investigations across diverse traffic.

INFRASTRUCTURE PROTECTION

Tenant hardening prescriptively configures operating systems to secure baselines against exploits through patches, signatures, and constraints. Virtual machine defenses leverage dedicated CPUs/RAM, avoiding overcommit risks. Encryption-at-rest preserves confidentiality if storage encounters disclosure. Disaster recovery strategies ensure durability by implementing geographical redundancy and failover testing. Immutable infrastructure avoids lateral impacts from compromises. Activity monitoring alerts anomalies proactively, whereas log consolidation offers forensic visibility.

APPLICATION SECURITY

Leverage web application firewalls and API gateways validating payloads centrally. Input sanitization avoids injection flaws, while output encoding protects rendering. Threat modeling guides protection focusing on risks. Secrets management anonymizes credentials, leveraging encryption wherever possible. Static/dynamic application security testing (SAST/DAST) identifies flaws before production, and penetration testing thereafter validates remediation work as planned. Runtime application self-protection monitors behaviors for attacks.

IDENTITY FEDERATION

Federated identity and access management (IAM) bridge authentication across providers, enabling single sign-on through standard protocols like SAML and OpenID Connect. Central authorization avoids credential sprawl, increasing manageability. Multi-factor authentication (MFA) strengthens logins for high-risk use cases. Audit logging offers accountability, while credential rotation maintains viability against information leakage over time. Seamless yet verified access improves user experience and compliance oversight.

DATA PROTECTION

Classification and labeling schemes guide handling according to sensitivity. Access zones constrain availability per need-to-know. Encryption protects confidentiality wherever stored, in use, or transmitted between regions/accounts. Keys remain secure under carefully managed roles through hardware security modules (HSMs). Automated data discovery and classification tools enforce policies continually as data flows change. Deletion renders information non-recoverable according to legal wipe standards.

CONFIGURATION MANAGEMENT

Secure configuration baselines applied via configuration-as-code limit attack surfaces and ensure consistent environments. Templates leverage infrastructure-as-code to model designs that are reviewable/reproducible. Drift detection alerts straying from standards while remediation returns compliance. Segments isolate production proving grounds.

VULNERABILITY MANAGEMENT

Vulnerability scanning discovers weaknesses before exploitation through credentials and authenticated agents for comprehensive views. Patching prioritizes according to risk factors. Penetration testing validates remediation work, while phishing simulations strengthen user vigilance.

LOGGING AND MONITORING

Centralized logging retains forensic evidence and detects anomalies across infrastructure layers. Analytics identify patterns warranting investigations through log management, SIEM, UEBA, and SOAR platforms. Automation reacts to indications proactively containing impacts.

SUPPLY CHAIN SECURITY

Vetting partners appraise development lifecycle and hosting security standards, while contractual agreements mandate vulnerability disclosure for a coordinated response. Licenses implement traditional software controls in the cloud. Build artifacts undergo integrity validation from repositories of record.

GOVERNANCE

The policy defines control objectives aligned with industry standards and regulations. Automated attestation confirms conformance through continuous authorization enforcing baselines. Change management procedures govern deployments through multiple approvals. Separation of duties prevents abuse across privileged roles operating services. Audits review program effectiveness, suggesting optimizations.

INCIDENT RESPONSE

Orchestrated containment and eradication plans enacted via runbooks put protections to the test under pressure. Restoration validates systems that resist recurrence while lessons are learned to evolve strategies. Training exercises validate abilities to respond to evolving scenarios.

BOOK 4
Endpoint Security and User Awareness

CHAPTER 13
Endpoint Security

Antivirus and Anti-Malware

Antivirus and anti-malware software play a crucial role in endpoint security. By detecting and blocking malware and other threats, these solutions help secure user devices from malicious attacks. This chapter will provide an in-depth look at antivirus and anti-malware, how they work, features to consider, and best practices for implementation and management.

WHAT ARE ANTIVIRUS AND ANTI-MALWARE?

Antivirus and anti-malware software both aim to protect devices from malware, but they differ slightly in focus and capabilities. Antivirus software primarily detects and removes computer viruses. Computer viruses are self-replicating programs that spread by inserting copies of themselves into other executable code or documents. Anti-malware takes a broader approach by also addressing other types of malicious software or potentially unwanted programs beyond just viruses. This includes things like worms, Trojans, ransomware, spyware, and adware. Most commercial antivirus and anti-malware solutions on the market today incorporate elements of both and provide layered defenses against a wide range of threats. For simplicity, the term antivirus will be used in this chapter to refer to these comprehensive endpoint security solutions.

HOW ANTIVIRUS WORKS

Antivirus utilizes several methods to identify and block malware:

Signature-Based Detection

Signature-based or signature scanning checks files and codes against a database of known malware signatures or fingerprints. Whenever new malware is identified, its signature is added to regularly updated antivirus definition files. This method is effective against previously discovered threats but cannot catch new or unknown viruses.

Heuristic/Behavioral Analysis

Heuristic or behavioral analysis monitors how programs operate and interact to detect abnormal or malicious behavior, even when exact signatures are unknown. It looks at things like attempts to disable security software, suspicious network activity, or signs of code injection.

Cloud-Based Threat Intelligence

Leveraging cloud-based global threat intelligence, sandboxing, and machine learning allows continuous analysis of emerging malware patterns and rapid identification of new outbreaks across a large user base. Unknown samples can be run safely in virtual environments to analyze behaviors.

TYPES OF ANTIVIRUS PROTECTION

Antivirus solutions protect endpoints through various integrated modules:

Real-Time Protection

Real-time or on-access scanning monitors file systems, processes, and program activity in real-time to detect viruses during regular use or downloads. It can automatically clean or quarantine detected threats.

Scheduled Scans

Scheduled full system scans run periodically to check the entire file system even when not actively accessing files.

On-Demand Scans

On-demand scans can be manually triggered at any time to check specific files, folders, or entire devices for existing infections.

Web Protection

Web protection filters harmful or infected websites and blocks drive-by malware downloads during web browsing and email activities.

Device Control

Device control manages the use of removable storage devices like USB drives by allowing or blocking access for data transfers to reduce infection risk.

KEY FEATURES TO CONSIDER

When choosing antivirus for an organization, key capabilities to evaluate include:
- Platform support for operating systems and servers in use
- Device support, including desktops, laptops, mobile devices
- Deployment options like a cloud-based console for centralized management
- Real-time protection, scheduled scans, on-demand scans
- Web protection, firewall, intrusion prevention, device control
- Automatic updates and definition file management
- Quarantine and rollback options for contained removal of detected threats
- Compatibility with other endpoint security solutions
- Performance impact and system resource usage
- Reporting functionality, audit logs, alerting
- support services, reliability of vendor

DEPLOYMENT

Careful planning is required to deploy anti-malware tools effectively. Start by identifying all systems that need protection - desktops, laptops, servers, databases, IoT devices, and mobile endpoints. Understand supported operating systems and applications to minimize compatibility issues. A phased rollout allows high-priority systems like servers to be protected first. Automate installations through a centralized management console for scalability. Integrate anti-malware with existing endpoint management, networking tools, and patch management systems. This provides consolidated visibility and control.

CONFIGURATION

Leverage the management interface to tailor scans and policies to business needs. Enable real-time protection and schedule scans to achieve the needed balance of thoroughness and performance.

Structure policies logically according to functions like mobile, office, and VPN. Apply strict enterprise baselines while allowing more relaxed custom profiles where risk is lower. Create centralized logging, reporting, alerts, and dashboards for holistic oversight. Establish credentials and access controls within the management platform.

SIGNATURE UPDATES

Routine signature updates are critical for detecting new malware variants. Configure daily downloads and automatic installation of definition packages. Deploy to a local update server in large environments for faster distribution. Supplement online signatures with offline packages on disconnected systems and during outages. Maintain version control across upgrades. Coordinate updates with related systems like firewalls or endpoints.

HEURISTICS AND BEHAVIORAL ANALYSIS

These techniques analyze file behaviors rather than relying solely on signatures. Enable machine learning and heuristic monitoring proportionate to resource tolerances. Tune sensitivity to balance detections and false positives. Apply stricter policies for sensitive assets while relaxing settings on typical workloads. Temporarily isolate detected files until analysis confirms a malware or false positive finding.

REPORTING AND ANALYTICS

Centralized logs and reports allow threat visibility and investigation. Capture alerts, blocked malware instances, and remediated vulnerabilities over time. Use analytics to gain strategic insights from trends. Visualize metrics through dashboards to optimize anti-malware controls and residual risks. Protect anonymity when benchmarking with peer organizations for additional context.

TRAINING AND SUPPORT

Educate users on compromise indications and how to use anti-malware tools properly through targeted training. Maintain knowledge bases and support portals to reinforce security practices among all levels of personnel. Promote escalation paths through expert support teams and software vendors for complex issues. Conduct simulated phishing tests to refine end-user education over time as techniques evolve.

INTEGRATION AND MAINTENANCE

Anti-malware complements other defenses when integrated properly. Link tools to firewalls, patch management systems, IDS/IPS sensors, and data loss prevention. Regularly evaluate configurations and maturity assessments to identify optimization opportunities. Document and test improvements transparently. Outsource management selectively to maintain oversight and realize cost efficiencies through experts. Continuous adaptation keeps protections aligned with the changing threat landscape.

Endpoint Security Solutions

Endpoint devices act as primary access points and hold valuable corporate assets, yet their portability outside secure networks introduces cyber risks. We will explore how endpoint security solutions enhance device defenses to restrict threats while enabling productivity. Comprehensive endpoint protection involves far more than basic antivirus.

ENDPOINT DETECTION AND RESPONSE

Endpoint detection and response (EDR) strengthens early threat detection capabilities. EDR agents deployed on endpoints continuously monitor processes, files, network connections, and other artifact changes using deep visibility techniques. They detect suspicious events like abnormal application launching, unusual outbound network requests, or unauthorized code and data transfers. Alerts flag potential compromises for manual review and automated response. Incident response is rapid through investigation tools that quarantine endpoints, terminate suspicious processes, and roll back changes to isolated incidents. Logging provides comprehensive visibility into historical endpoint activities and events for forensic root cause analysis.

NEXT-GENERATION ANTIVIRUS

While traditional anti-malware aims at known threats through signature matching, next-generation antivirus (NGAV) layers on proactive unknown threat prevention strategies. NGAV solutions still provide anti-malware engines and scanning but also integrate behavior-blocking technologies like application whitelisting, memory exploitation prevention, and machine learning models. By analyzing process behaviors, application executions, and system changes, NGAV detects malware masquerading as white processes and unknown fileless attacks lacking signatures. It stops previously unseen malicious behaviors in real-time before damage occurs through behavioral sandboxing and artificial intelligence (AI). Combined signature and behavioral views deliver multi-layered protections.

APPLICATION CONTROL

Application control regulates approved software and prevents unassessed programs from running. Whitelisting models define a list of trusted applications verified as secure and necessary for business functions. Any unrecognized program is denied automatically. This prevents untrusted and unsecured software from being used maliciously or accidentally for cyberattacks. Whitelisting models regularly review new applications for inclusion and remove unsupported or unneeded legacy programs. They reduce the sprawling software ecosystem to a vetted minimum, simplifying assurance of secure configurations. Combined with EDR for anomalous behavior monitoring, application control strengthens access controls.

DEVICE CONTROL AND ENCRYPTION

Device control establishes policies governing external storage device access, like USB drives, according to data sensitivity. Options include read-only, auto-execution blocking, file type restrictions, watermarking, and full-disk encryption (FDE) when drives are attached. Policies apply consistently across desktop, laptop, and mobile endpoints using centralized management. FDE protects saved files and entire disk volumes with robust encryption, which is impossible for attackers to bypass if devices are lost or stolen. Policy-based conditional access encrypts removable media automatically on connection according to classification. Further protections include a boot disk, endpoint file/folder, and in-transit encryption. Encryption establishes a robust last line of defense for data at rest and in use.

ENDPOINT SECURITY SUITES

Endpoint security suites offer consolidated next-generation protection in single-agent architectures for simplified coordination and management at scale. Entry-level suites integrate antivirus, personal firewall, file encryption, and basic device control/policies in one agent. Mid-tier suites add full-featured EDR, threat-hunting dashboards, NGAV, and application control modules. Advanced suites couple comprehensive endpoint, network, and identity security stacks through a unified console. Unified endpoint management (UEM) combinations smoothly govern diverse endpoints as one centrally secured fleet.

BYOD Policies

As remote and hybrid work models increase in popularity, more employees utilize personal devices for work purposes through bring-your-own-device (BYOD) programs. While BYOD enables flexibility, it also introduces risk if not properly governed. A logical BYOD policy is necessary to securely enable productive mixed-use of personal devices on company networks and systems.

POLICY PURPOSE AND OBJECTIVES

The BYOD policy clearly outlines its intent to accommodate approved personal devices for business activities in a risk-managed manner, balancing security, compliance, and usability. Core objectives establish guidelines for addressing overlapping personal and professional responsibilities on shared devices, protecting corporate assets and data, ensuring network safety, and meeting regulatory obligations. Considerations for ongoing policy evaluation and improvement are included.

DEVICE ELIGIBILITY AND REGISTRATION

Eligible device types based on technical capabilities and platforms are defined, such as laptops or smartphones running specific operating systems and security levels. A formal registration process requiring forms and device configurations establishes user consent to policy rules. Inventorying BYOD assets improves incident response and informs technical controls. Data deletion responsibilities upon employee separation are addressed.

ACCEPTABLE USE STANDARDS

Standards restricting unsafe behaviors are outlined, including separating business and personal activities; prohibiting unlawful, unethical, or dangerous activities; protecting passwords and credentials; practicing responsible, respectful communication; and respecting software licenses and copyrights. Procedures for incidents or policy breaches are detailed.

SECURITY REQUIREMENTS

Baseline technical controls around a secure installation posture are mandated, such as endpoint protection, regularly patched operating systems, whole-disk encryption, strong passwords, automatic screen locks, and remote malware detection/removal capabilities. Device ownership responsibilities for maintaining updates are defined. Continuous compliance requirements are specified.

RISK ACKNOWLEDGMENT

The possibility of reputational or legal issues from improper usage, as well as limitations of organizational liability for personal devices or data, are clarified through sign-off. Restrictions on certain high-risk activities involve an acknowledgment of associated dangers. Security exemption requests and approval guidelines exist.

ACCESS MANAGEMENT

Access methods securely authenticate users and devices, including multifactor authentication and certificate enrollment. Authorization controls section policies define suitable access to resource types. Separation techniques establish partitions between managed business applications and personal activities. Continuous monitoring policies outline management tools and regular diagnostics.

DATA HANDLING STANDARDS

Corporate data classification and protection protocols determine allowed use and storage locations. Controls prevent business asset leakage from BYODs, including storage encryption, network segregation, and transmission security. Mechanisms address data backups, retention, and deletion responsibilities at endpoint decommissioning.

COMPLIANCE MEASURES

Applicable industry or national privacy regulations in contexts like finance or healthcare are identified and mapped to technical safeguards. Audit preparations involve record-keeping of BYOD assets and activity along with incident documentation procedures. Monitoring and logging substantiate continuous compliance and policy enforcement techniques.

SUPPORT AND ENFORCEMENT

Support options and timeframes for assistance clarify self-service capabilities. An approval workflow governs compliant applications. Non-compliance consequences define corrective actions and access revocation processes with escalation routes. Periodic reviews ensure policy efficacy for an evolving landscape while protecting corporate value.

BYOD PROGRAM LAUNCH

The roll-out addresses change management with advanced communication, registration deadlines, and technical requirements education. Pilot testing vets policy manageability. Gradual scaling permits refinements. Adequate resources establish oversight and enforcement. Change readiness assessments monitor adherence longitudinally with the agility to update rules prudently.

TECHNICAL CONFIGURATION

Baseline hardening requirements are mandated through centrally managed mobile device management (MDM) and mobile application management (MAM) platforms. System-level controls include firewalls, antivirus, automatic OS/app updates, password/pin locks, and remote wiping functionality. MDM establishes enrollment into a secured container, segregating personal and corporate profiles and applications. Selective installation and configurations apply policies according to data sensitivity. App protection restricts managed applications from accessing certain APIs. Restrictions and monitoring govern camera, encryption, locations, and network device usage.

DATA LOSS PREVENTION

Corporate information remains separated and encrypted using containerization technologies. Network segregation disciplines only allow suitable access. Leakage controls detect and prevent cut/paste into personal services. Digital rights management applies time-bound access and permission controls for controlled distribution. Accessible storage segregation technically partitions protected business files.

COMPLIANCE VERIFICATION

Inventory records verify enrolled devices' compliance posture through remote scans. Investigative tools facilitate on-device forensics during audits or incidents. Automated reports document policy exceptions, non-compliance instances, and remediation timelines. Audit log retention satisfies records preservation mandates.

GOVERNANCE OVERSIGHT

Policy administrators review rule deviations and apply consistent enforcement. The approval workflow assesses devices and applications for risk. Access suspension addresses unmitigated vulnerabilities while coaching remediation. Disciplinary processes define consequences proportionate to severity and intent. Escalation procedures route unresolved matters appropriately.

TRAINING AND CULTURE

Onboarding material socializes program objectives and individual responsibilities early. Periodic reminders maintain awareness of changing tactics. Knowledge assessments evaluate comprehension. Positive reinforcement recognizes stakeholders, further enabling the policy spirit. A support desk handles routine queries efficiently and courteously.

CONTINUOUS IMPROVEMENT

Post-rollout observations assess usability, productivity impact, and oversight effectiveness. Surveys and interviews gather user sentiment. Analytics discern policy gaps. Issues and enhancements are addressed through joint operational and policy reviews. Maturity assessments benchmark progress against objectives. Flexibility maintains security as technologies evolve cooperatively over time.

CHAPTER 14
User Training and Awareness

Social Engineering Awareness

As cyber criminals increasingly rely on manipulating human behaviors, social engineering poses serious risks. However, awareness training can strengthen defenses by educating employees to identify common manipulation tactics and resist triggering unintended security lapses. This chapter discusses the importance of social engineering awareness programs and best practices for effective implementation.

UNDERSTANDING SOCIAL ENGINEERING

Social engineering involves psychologically deceiving individuals into performing actions or revealing sensitive information through misleading conversations. It preys on natural human tendencies to be helpful, make social connections, and avoid conflict. Attackers gather personal details to assume trusted personas and spin convincing narratives, triggering instinctive trusting responses. Understanding why social engineering works helps counter its power.

IMPACT OF SOCIAL ENGINEERING

Left unopposed, social engineering threatens confidentiality, integrity, and availability. It enables unauthorized access to networks, systems, and data through stolen credentials or persuaded insiders. Manipulation for fraudulent financial gain or reputational damage also occurs. Compromised users unknowingly spread malware or expose vulnerabilities from socially engineered mistakes. Even inadvertent security slips created or worsened by social manipulation require remediation costs. Clearly, social engineering awareness bolsters the last line of human defense, weakening risks from social deception tactics.

TRAINING GOALS AND FOCUS AREAS

The goal of social engineering awareness training is to familiarize employees with common manipulation techniques, teach skeptical habits, and establish protocols for handling suspicious requests. Focus areas include recognizing pretexting to establish false trust, identifying deception tactics, skepticism of emotional appeals, verifying uncertain requests up lines of responsibility, and reporting anomalous requests. The training aims to raise consciousness of one's own instincts vulnerable to exploitation, not cast suspicion on fellow employees. It imparts practical judgment rather than accusation when encountering possibly engineered situations requiring validation. Overall, the objective is cultivating an inquisitive mindset that is better able to discern truth from skilled social deception.

DESIGNING EFFECTIVE TRAINING

Training programs prove most impactful using evidence-based methods. Varied interactive exercises stimulate engagement beyond passive content consumption. Regular reinforcement solidifies the retention of lessons over time. Programs incorporate real social engineering attempt examples and case studies to resonate. Hands-on activities place participants in engineered hypothetical scenarios requiring skeptical analysis and sound decision-making. Formats like role play, puzzles, or games invite active problem-solving. Assessing understanding through facilitated discussion and knowledge testing ensures comprehension. Prompting participants to identify personal vulnerabilities further cements learning.

PREPARING THE LEARNING ENVIRONMENT

Leadership support for training signifies its importance to the organization. Instructors require expertise in both social engineering techniques and adult learning methods. A safe, inclusive environment invites open participation and questioning. Clear expectations address the sensitive nature of social engineering without judgment or embarrassment. Confidentiality preserves anonymity when practicing scenarios. Reasonable time allocation, breaks, and interactive elements maintain engagement. Accessible virtual and physical logistics expand reach. These environment fundamentals optimize receptiveness to the material.

REINFORCEMENT AND CONTINUAL IMPROVEMENT

Sustained reinforcement strengthens the retention of awareness over time. Refresher courses address evolving tactics, while accelerated learning incorporates situational experiences back into future pieces of training. Post-training evaluations identify gaps to refine content and delivery. Supplemental methods like newsletter tips, posters, or rewards for modeled behavior maintain top-of-mind vigilance. Reporting anonymized social engineering attempts received for lessons learned boosts analysis and continual education program improvement. Long-term reinforcement through various means embeds durable habits superior to isolated, one-off sessions.

METRICS AND TRACKING

Collecting social engineering metrics illustrates program value. Tracking attempted manipulation reports, awareness training completions, simulated test results, and identified response gaps through surveys demonstrates progress and highlights remaining work. Comparing pre-post training knowledge, attitude, and intended behavior changes validates impact. Incident investigations ascertain root causes and identify any education lapses contributing to breaches for course corrective actions. Overlaying metrics with security data like phishing click rates indicates awareness translation into reduced risks. Regular communications synthesize metrics to showcase the evolution and needs of leadership and participants.

PRACTICAL CONSIDERATIONS

Budgeting appropriately funds high-quality regular training, simulated tests, and overtime for quality improvement efforts. Secure learning management systems schedule, track completions, and house supplemental materials. Accessibility accommodates diverse learners. Instructors require social engineering experience and adult learning certifications. Leadership sponsorship boosts participation and accountability. Respecting time constraints avoids education fatigue with focused, lively sessions. Policies integrate training mandates and response protocols. Support references resolve uncertainty respectfully.

Phishing Detection and Prevention

As phishing attacks grow increasingly sophisticated and targeted, combating this pervasive social engineering threat demands a layered defense strategy. It explores technical detection and prevention techniques, as well as policy and training approaches that together diminish phishing's impact. While no single measure provides complete protection, an integrated program guards against both known and unknown phishing risks.

TECHNICAL DETECTION

Technical detection tools examine email content and execution behavior to flag phishing attempts based on characteristics correlated with deception. Spam filters identify messages containing triggers like poor grammar, undisclosed recipients, or suspicious URLs to quarantine before delivery. Heuristic analyses evaluate message elements for impersonation likelihood through scans of branding, wording, webpage links, and embedded images against known organization standards. Machine learning models also detect anomalies in senders, words, formatting, or attachment file types compared to a user's regular correspondence profile.

BLOCKLISTING AND WHITELISTING

Sending IP reputation services blocks or challenges messages from historically abusive domains while allowing known organization IPs unfettered access through IP whitelisting in mail transfer agent (MTA) configurations. Whitelists safeguard legitimate correspondence, while catch-all traps diversify risk beyond individual sources. On the recipient side, browser blacklists halt drive-by downloads from shady sites while whitelisting enterprise applications assuredly updates from approved locations. Application control reinforces these access rules to contain potential infection avenues. Together, source reputation and recipient safe lists strengthen static perimeter defenses.

DMARC/DKIM EMAIL AUTHENTICATION

Domain-based Message Authentication, Reporting and Conformance (DMARC), and DomainKeys Identified Mail (DKIM) standards help validate authentic senders through cryptographic email authentication. DMARC enforces and reports on mail sender alignment between message header and domain, while DKIM signs each message to verify the originating server identity upon receipt. Their deployment across legitimate domains elevates prevention compared to the opportunistic forging of trusted names. When paired with Sender Policy Framework (SPF) records documenting permitted sending hosts, authentication standards raise the bar on impersonating valid correspondents.

URL SHORTENER MONITORING

Since phishing payloads commonly hide behind URL shorteners, services monitor all shortened links in real-time to detect and block malicious destinations before users click through. By decoding shortened URLs, malicious payloads are revealed and blocked at the redirection phase versus relying on users to avoid the final landing page. URL transparency closes a manipulation channel.

TARGETED EDUCATION AND TRAINING

While technical controls detect much phishing, a well-designed training program strengthens individual judgment when technical solutions are bypassed. Proper email security hygiene and behavioral best practices prevent employee endangerment. Targeted modules explore prevalent ploys like impersonation, urgency tricks, and deception indicators within messages and websites. Hands-on exercises placed participants in engineered scenarios requiring skepticism to cultivate decision-making muscle memory. Knowledge testing and impact surveys verify comprehension and long-term retention over time. Simulated phishing tests periodically probe individual resilience respectfully to identify where education requires reinforcement without punitive intent. Adjusting training based on such practical assessments maximizes preparation against real attacks.

POLICY AND PROCESS

Email and web usage policies define access expectations and detail how to report possibly malicious messages following response trees. Uncertainty mandates caution rather than reckless clicking. Procedures address spam incorrectly delivered through false positives as well to preclude valid correspondence deletion anxiety. Special handling protocols expedite incident analysis upon actual compromise reports. Support references for validating suspect messages establish respectful means of avoiding embarrassment when unsure. Integrating socialized policy and process strengthens the fabric of preventative habits in all participants over time.

METRICS AND OVERSIGHT

To evidence program value, collecting quantitative metrics tracks improvement. Metrics capture simulated test failures declining with training, actual phishing reports blocked or submitted for analysis, risky user behaviors measured through email security platforms, and known phishing infrastructure takedowns thwarting future attacks. Comparing pre-post training understanding and intended behaviors demonstrates impact. Correlating such security data to real security events like malware infections indicates effective risk reduction translation. Detailed metrics substantiate the program's worth to leadership and areas still requiring focus for protection evolution.

User Behavior Analytics

As cyberattacks evolve, detecting threats from anomalous user activity has become crucial. User behavior analytics (UBA) utilizes machine learning to establish digital user-profiles and pinpoint abnormal deviations indicative of compromised accounts or insider threats.

MODELING NORMAL BEHAVIOR

UBA platforms ingest logs of various user actions - login locations, application access patterns, file interactions, and more - to learn typical behaviors over time using unsupervised machine learning algorithms. Models distinguish unique characteristics like time-of-day access tendencies or common document co-editing. Abnormal variations from the established baseline warrant investigation as potential security concerns.

USE CASES FOR DETECTION

UBA detects threats its logs contain evidence of by comparing real-time user actions to baseline profiles. Deviation flagging includes Spotting insider threats slowly occurring under the radar.

INVESTIGATION AND RESPONSE

When alerts fire, case management dashboards present contextual evidence and related event timelines to security teams. Events may indicate actual threats requiring a swift response or false alarms from legitimate unusual usage requiring exemption. Analysts contact flagged users respectfully to determine the cause to either remediate risks or update normal baselines incorporating new usage patterns.

MONITORING PRIVILEGED ACCOUNTS

Administrators and power users' profiles cover extensive normal activities, so minor unique variations rarely trigger alerts versus typical end users. However, these privileged accounts warrant closer scrutiny due to their far-reaching capabilities. Reducing blind spots involves tailoring administrator behavior baselines narrowly and monitoring entitlement reviews.

IMPLEMENTATION ROADMAP

Selecting quality log sources suitable for modeling and integrating them into UBA platforms establishes foundational visibility. Change management garners support by socializing how it strengthens rather than weakens privacy through contextual investigation of actual abnormalities. Expertise develops over time through ongoing tuning informed by experience analyzing real incidents. Metrics also help optimize by evaluating which detections translated to real issues or required discarding. Gradually expanding monitored scopes and enriching data sources over multiple phases accomplishes UBA implementation prudently according to capacity. Regular program reviews point to maturation opportunities.

ADDRESSING PRIVACY CONCERNS

Anonymizing personally identifiable information mitigates privacy exposure when UBA evidence becomes relevant in audits or litigation. Destruction policies ensure data use strictly for its originally intended security purpose rather than unrelated profiling. Evaluating model biases using representative control groups and decrypting questionable detections to verify circumstantial evidence also builds trust. With oversight, UBA need not compromise privacy to strengthen security.

PREPARING THE ENVIRONMENT

For the UBA program's success, leadership sponsoring establishes expectations, whereas change management addresses acceptance. Accountability measures avoid potential function creep into unchartered territories. Supporting policies define logging requirements and response protocols aligned with broader security operations. Resource availability funds are needed to log aggregation, normalization, and analytics platform infrastructure according to processing loads. Experienced data scientists implement UBA program design through configuration, tuning, and expansion phases. Succession plans account for knowledge transfers if roles change to maintain capabilities. Legal and compliance advisors consult on privacy and regulatory mandates.

EDUCATING STAKEHOLDERS

User education clarifies the benefit of UBA detection mechanisms versus hypothetical privacy impedance. The material emphasizes its role in strengthening rather than weakening account security through abnormality investigation alone. Buy-in surveys evaluate understanding, while knowledge assessments verify comprehension over time. Accountability reassures proper usage through auditing.

ANALYST TRAINING

Detection analysts receive UBA platform certification involving proficiency in statistical anomaly detection techniques, user modeling, case management navigation, and respectful interactions. Ongoing skill development occurs through technology updates, emerging risks education, and experience gained reviewing actual abnormal incidents and exposure to edge cases. Responders are equipped to maximize UBA potential and represent the program professionally.

METRICS AND OPTIMIZATION

Quantitative metrics such as detection accuracy, model coverage, closed cases, and response times demonstrate oversight. Qualitative feedback from investigations, user surveys, and privacy assessments identifies areas for refinement. Observability augments investigations with context for expedited resolution. Regular model evaluations catch concept drift, potentially degrading effectiveness. Optimization ensures that UBA continually strengthens security practices through data.

THIRD-PARTY UBA

For immature programs or budget limitations, managed services provide temporary outsourced UBA capabilities. However, insights isolated from an organization's context may undermine third parties' efficacy. Controls ensure data and detections strictly serve their original security purpose according to agreements. Bring-your-own-analytics eventually replaces transitional outsourcing when internal expertise matures.

CHAPTER 15
Insider Threat Detection and Mitigation

Insider Threat Indicators

While outsider attacks pose serious risks, well-resourced insiders exploiting authorized access present distinct challenges. We'll explore indicators that insider threat programs detect to identify concerning behaviors warranting investigation before harm occurs. A multi-faceted approach considers technical, administrative, and behavioral signs that are adjustable based on changing risks.

TECHNICAL ACTIVITY MONITORING

Monitoring user activities provides objective data. Examining account access trends, file interactions, application usage patterns, and network behaviors pinpoints anomalies contradicting usual job functions. Deviations warrant vetting, such as file transfers exceeding roles during non-work hours or accessing numerous sensitive documents recently. However, technical monitoring alone leaves context lacking.

POLICIES AND USER AGREEMENTS

Clearly communicated policies regarding authorized access establish expectations upfront, while user agreements require annual acknowledgment. Special access approvals, entitlement reviews, and policy deviation reporting formalize procedures. When selectively excluding personal system accesses unimportant to insider threat, the scope remains focused on work roles and systems.

PRIVILEGED USER OVERSIGHT

Heightened monitoring applies to high-impact accounts due to its far-reaching capabilities. Baseline privileged user activities establish clearer abnormality definitions. Approval workflows involve manager reviews, whereas periodic testing assesses compliance. However, cultural sensitivity retains trusting relationships, avoiding perceptions as "big brother".

BEHAVIORAL INDICATORS

Profile questionnaires and interviews identify potential motivators weighing on employees. Combining subjective tips from coworkers' and managers' observations detects behavioral changes like conflicts, disengagement signs concerning workplace conduct, or suspicious questioning. Financial difficulties correlate but require discretion - context determines significance.

INVESTIGATION TECHNIQUES

Abnormalities warrant vetting, whether technical, situational, or behavioral in nature. Threat intelligence and open-source research explore public records for financial troubles, criminal charges concerning associates, or online statements. Voluntary interviews invite explanations for flagged activities, respectfully seeking understanding versus accusation.

RESOLUTION AND SUPPORT

Most flagged issues prove innocuous and can be resolved through transparency. However, validated cases involving policy non-compliance or insider risks activate response plans through coordination with HR and legal according to severity. Support references aim to retain trustworthy employees whenever possible through confidential assistance.

PROGRAM SOCIALIZATION

Executive backing socializes the program as protecting mission-critical resources rather than "spying". Awareness materials clarify differentiated monitoring domains and respect for personal lives. As insider threats often emerge gradually, social support also establishes approachability to diffuse tensions before they escalate. However, consistent oversight deters damaging behaviors.

METRICS AND TRACKING

Metrics substantiate the program by evaluating risk identification and mature resolution processes over time. Examples include flagged incidents closed through understanding versus discipline, intelligence gathered from open sources, training completion rates, and average response times. Qualitative feedback from investigations and interviews also provides perspective. Correlating detections to real insider-related events—such as data exfiltration timelines originating internally—validates accumulated and applied contextual understanding. The statistical analysis identifies the most common indicators requiring focus or edge cases necessitating deeper exploration. Regular tracking showcases progress and upcoming needs.

CONTINUAL IMPROVEMENT

Since insider risk factors evolve with macro trends, the program likewise dynamically refines. Periodic maturity assessments benchmark against objectives and processes compared to peer programs. Surveys gather perceptions, while discussions extract lessons from past reviews and cases. Updated policies integrate legislative and organizational changes. Reinforcement maintains comprehensive understandings as skills evolve. Documentation records program revisions transparently for oversight and succession. Privacy impact assessments identify sensitive data exposures warranting minimization. Insights from actual issues inform adjusting monitoring scopes, interview questions, and response procedures proportionally based on updated contextual factors. Responsible optimization keeps protections current.

STAKEHOLDERS AND COMMUNICATION

Most critical, executive support backs program necessity balanced with cultural and legal sensitivities. Perspectives from HR, facilities, security, and legal advisors shape effective design and operation. Progress communications earn trust through transparency on goals, protecting all parties honestly and fairly according to policies, and acknowledging understanding. Regular forums invite feedback-strengthening approaches cooperatively over time.

Monitoring Employee Activities

As remote and hybrid work grow prevalent, organizations require visibility into workplace tools and systems usage. However, monitoring generates privacy concerns if mishandled. We will discuss technical and policy strategies for carrying out activity oversight respectfully and productively within legal compliance. When implemented judiciously, monitoring strengthens security and productivity without compromising trust.

ESTABLISHING OBJECTIVES

Before deploying tools, define explicit monitoring purposes aligned with responsibilities like ensuring appropriate access, detecting policy violations, and investigating security issues – not general surveillance. Intended uses to maintain a narrow operational focus versus mission creep, preserving oversight legitimacy to stakeholders. Documentation substantiates obligations met proportionally.

SELECTING MONITORING TOOLS

Choosing platforms collect only relevant activity metadata, not personally sensitive files or keystrokes. Systems observe authorized access locations, application types used, website categories visited, and file interactions while avoiding passwords or verbatim communications. Limited recording windows balanced with data protection prevent indefinite retention, preserving privacy.

CONTROLLING TOOL CONFIGURATIONS

Granular controls configure which user groups, system types, and activity categories require oversight proportional to roles versus blanket tracking. Settings selectively exclude approved personal assets and activities wherever job duties permit. System health and maintenance rather than vague "productivity" goals justify technical monitoring extents to stakeholders.

UPDATING ACCESS POLICIES

Access and acceptable use policies receive revisions incorporating expanded visibility necessitating informed consent. Procedural documentation records approved tools, scopes, data retention schedules, and investigatory procedures meeting compliance and proportionality requirements. Policy acknowledgments protect all parties through transparency on changed expectations.

INCIDENT RESPONSE

Protocols define flagged activity escalation paths involving stakeholders impartially evaluating circumstantial explanations. Unjustified accesses provoke disciplinary actions proportional to severity and intent through documented processes respecting employee rights. Direct oversight aims to resolve concerns versus accusations, maintaining trust.

PRIVACY BY DESIGN

Monitoring preservation, access controls, and data destruction practices embed privacy into program design from inception. Anonymizing sensitive personal details avoids function creep risks. Program assessments identify exposures necessitating minimization through diligent documentation, testing, and stakeholder feedback.

SOCIALIZING THE PROGRAM

To establish transparency and gain support, communication strategies clarify monitoring purposes, scoping safeguards, and redress avenues to affected populations. Clear justifications counter potential "Big Brother" perceptions through open forums, training materials, and policy review touchpoints. User awareness fosters understanding of roles versus personal lives.

METRICS AND PROGRAM IMPROVEMENT

Regularly tracking metrics like incident detection rates, timeliness metrics, and closed case volumes indicate areas requiring focus over time. Gathering user sentiment through surveys identifies undesirable impacts necessitating mitigation. Analytics uncover new risk patterns meriting attention or unused capabilities deserving optimization. Periodic reviews benchmark maturity against evolving best practices. Documentation records program revisions transparently. Assessments identify exposure risks necessitating minimization through diligent documentation, testing, and feedback.

GOVERNANCE AND OVERSIGHT

Oversight committees involving representatives from IT, HR, Legal, and Employee Relations evaluate monitoring procedures and investigate concerns impartially. Program administrators convey intended benefits transparently through open-access portals. Auditable controls safeguard data from unauthorized access, while litigation holds support review processes meeting compliance standards.

THIRD-PARTY CONSIDERATIONS

Outsourcing some monitoring responsibilities involves third parties bound by service-level agreements governing tool configurations, data access protocols, and incident response coordination. Vendor risk assessments evaluate providers' security, privacy, and record management practices, ensuring outsourced capabilities align with internal program design principles and obligations.

Responding to Insider Threats

While preventing insider risks entirely remains challenging, containing damages requires swift, nuanced response strategies. We will discuss approaches for addressing insider threat incidents judiciously according to severity determined through investigations, respecting all parties' privacy and legal rights. Sensitivity mitigates tensions through proportionality.

PLANNING THE RESPONSE

Cross-functional response plans outline communication protocols, escalation paths, containment procedures, and digital/physical evidence handling according to applicable policies and jurisdictional regulations. Pre-assigning Incident Response Teams comprised of HR, IT, Facilities, and Legal ensures coordinated preparedness for various scenarios. Mappings of key contacts, their roles, and escalation protocols are easily accessible for real incidents. Response playbooks consolidate standardized procedures, external contacts, and external communications guidance according to the level and nature of incidents. Careful planning of all aspects of response handling helps to efficiently and sensitively manage real issues according to pre-determined best practices when they do occur.

INITIATING RESPONSE

Flagged incidents warrant prompt vetting through open source and system access reviews, respectfully exploring anomalous behaviors or motivations with the involved individual. If concerning data departures indicate policy violations or risks, escalation to IR Teams establishes secondary containment, preventing exacerbation. For minor technical issues, containment may simply involve changing credentials or reviewing logs. More serious breaches could involve limiting all network or system access until a full investigation is conducted. Direct communication maintains transparency with any involved individuals while risks are assessed. Isolation of systems or changing of credentials for high-risk issues happens rapidly to prevent further data loss or compromises.

CONTAINMENT MEASURES

Proportional containment prevents data exfiltration or destruction according to potential damages indicated. Options include limiting network/system access, changing credentials, confiscating devices, or simply monitoring pending investigation outcomes to avoid the assumption of guilt. Direct communication maintains transparency. Stronger containment options like full system isolation or device confiscation require higher approval levels and have privacy implications. Less restrictive options focus on limiting specific access or monitoring behavior changes. Overall, the principle of proportionality based on the apparent level of risk helps minimize overreaction while still protecting sensitive data and systems.

CONDUCTING INVESTIGATIONS

Thorough, impartial collection of technical and interview evidence according to agreed procedures evaluates all sides to verify allegations. Where admission or forensic proof confirms violations, documented discussions determine the next proportional steps upholding individual protections cooperatively. Contextual details from interviews help in interpretation. Digital forensics requires careful chain of custody preservation. Interviews maintain respect and objectivity. Interpretations remain open pending full fact collection. As more details emerge, the next steps, like disciplinary action versus coaching, become clearer. However, assumptions are avoided until a full understanding based on all evidence emerges from transparent processes.

RESOLVING CONFIRMED ISSUES

Valet confirmed policy non-compliance or misuse with associated individuals respectfully through coaching or disciplinary actions proportionate to intent and impact according to agreed processes involving HR/Legal. Mitigation or removal avenues require considering the likelihood of recurring while preserving individual dignity to avoid distrust escalation. For less serious policy violations, options like coaching, reminders of expectations, or accessing counseling services may suffice compared to formal disciplinary actions. Mitigation strategies also assess technical or procedural controls requiring adjustment. Ultimately, resolution maintains a positive culture and cooperation through difficult discussions.

CRISIS COMMUNICATIONS

For significant damages necessitating external notification, coordinated statements disclose essential details and contain success succinctly according to transparency and privacy obligations. Appreciation for cooperation maintains positive relationships critical to future collaboration through difficult situations. Strong consideration of privacy and other legal constraints requires input from relevant departments. External updates balance disclosure of essential containment details with sensitivity to any involved individuals. Thanking cooperation reinforces a collaborative culture, even in crises, through transparency and care for all stakeholders.

AFTER ACTION REVIEW

Post-incident documentation and "lessons learned" discussions involving key response participants identify successes, gaps, and areas for enhancement according to impartial reviews. Findings prioritize technical, process, and coordination improvements in feeding preparedness updates. Participant feedback maintains employee voice, promoting continuous evolution. Comprehensive documentation and review involving all teams and perspectives help refine plans and strengthen future response handling. Addressing areas needing improvement maintains focus on progress over blame.

INDIVIDUAL SUPPORT CONSIDERATIONS

Sensitivity guides addressing concerns from bystanders exposed. Counseling availability supports psychological well-being, while confidential discussions clarify future expectations according to cultural sensitivities. Mitigation salvages relationships, avoiding distrust escalations wherever reasonably possible through transparency according to proportionality principles.

METRICS AND CONTINUOUS IMPROVEMENT

Defined metrics track response performance according to indicators like incident severity ratings, escalation times, containment effectiveness, issues recurrence, closure rates, and participant sentiment. Regular assessments identify policy, process, or technological optimizations responsively balancing care, controls, and cultural factors. Documentation informs evolution. Tracking containment speed, issue recurrence, and other quantifiable factors shows enhancements. Surveys and interviews evaluate participant experience to refine roles, communication, and coordination. Assessments involve cross-functional discussions to get different perspectives and identify inter-departmental optimization opportunities.

THIRD-PARTY EXTENSION

Supply chain extensions promote applying insider risk principles to business partners through contractual requirements around controls, screening, and oversight coordination. Joint tabletop simulations coordinate inter-organizational response coordination under shared responsibility models. Compatibility maintains protections comprehensively. Extending response coordination and periodic assessment to suppliers and other strategic partners helps close inter-organizational gaps. Contractual terms establish baseline controls and notification roles for each party. Simulated incidents test communication paths, escalation procedures, and collaboration across organizational boundaries. Bringing key suppliers into planning ensures that the response aligns beyond internal systems.

INTERNATIONAL COORDINATION

Harmonizing response frameworks across borders according to cultural norms and regulations addressing incidents involving multiple legal jurisdictions requires input navigation facilitating cooperation and escalation protocols. Understanding sensitivities optimizes resolution according to accountability, individual dignity, and respect wherever operations span boundaries. Incidents transiting international networks introduce jurisdictional complexities. Navigating varied regulations and cultural viewpoints demands extensive input. Connecting international incident notification authorities and clarifying information sharing allows understanding to develop.

PREVENTION INTEGRATION

Lessons reinforce tailored user awareness, credential management, access controls, anomaly monitoring, and strengthening layered protections against future recurrence. Focusing response enhanced through cooperation maintains a positive, learning-oriented culture, augmenting other initiatives holistically. With the understanding gained from incidents, targeted awareness, technical safeguards, and policy tightening aims to "design out" recurrence risk. Adjustments might enhance login verification, restrict removable media, or refine role-based access. Monitoring rule tuning detects concerning behaviors earlier. Promoting cooperation over discipline reinforces culture, viewing response as an opportunity rather than a punitive exercise.

CHAPTER 16
Security Compliance and Auditing

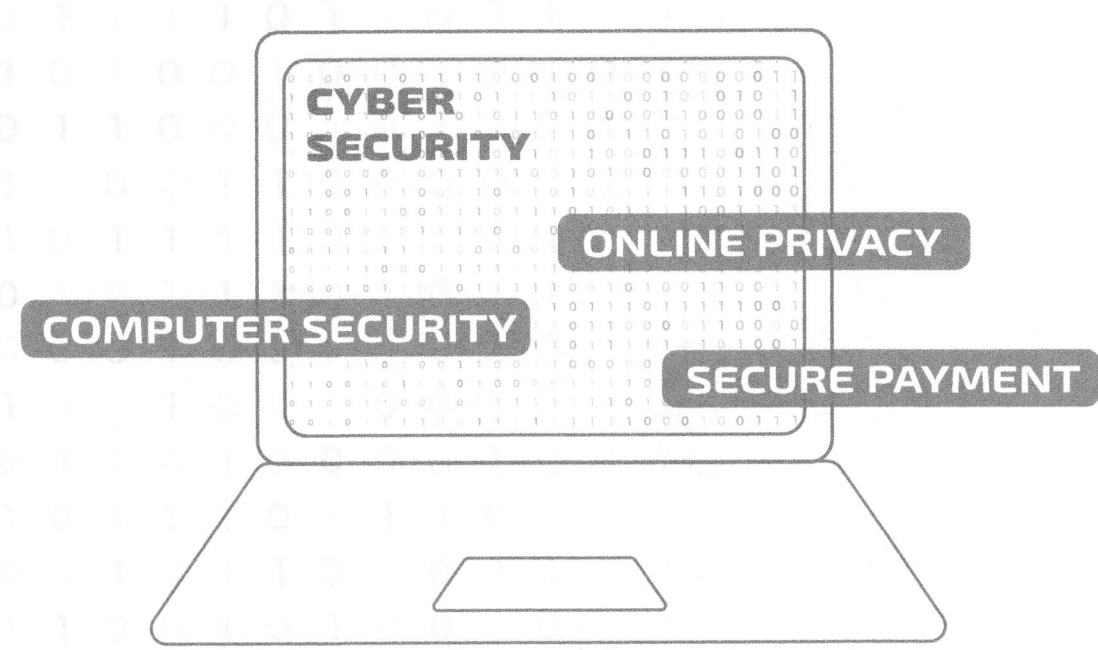

Regulatory Compliance

As digitization increases, organizations face stringent cybersecurity and data protection regulations. We will explore approaches for establishing robust regulatory compliance programs aligning operations with evolving mandates. Through preparation, documentation, and continual improvement, compliance contributes to responsible data stewardship while mitigating risks of punitive non-compliance.

ASSESSING REGULATORY LANDSCAPE

The first step involves mapping relevant regulations based on industry, location of operations, and data processing, such as privacy laws, security frameworks, and sector-specific requirements. Legal experts analyze obligations around secure systems, breach reporting, third-party risk management, and individual rights. Internationalization complicates varying jurisdictional standards necessitating navigation.

DOCUMENTATION AND CONTROLS

Formal documentation demonstrates adherence through policies, standards, reference materials, procedures, and defined roles meeting obligations. Technical, administrative, and physical controls align systems and practices, such as access restrictions, encryption, and auditing. Vendor contracts obligate suppliers to protect data according to agreements. Impact assessments evaluate controls, risks, and remediation measures periodically.

ONGOING AUDITING AND TESTING

Regular internal audits, 3rd party assessments, and compliance testing validate control effectiveness, procedural due diligence, vendor oversight, and response preparedness objectively against benchmarks. Findings prioritize remediating weaknesses and preventing non-compliance. Validation promotes a continuous improvement culture beyond check listing obligations.

TRAINING AND AWARENESS

All personnel receive role-specific training on compliance responsibilities and information security best practices tailored to job functions through diverse delivery methods ensuring understanding. Refresher modules address emerging requirements and risks. Simulated phishing programs test comprehension and resilience, strengthening cultural commitment.

INCIDENT RESPONSE

Crisp incident response plans coordinated by cross-functional teams outline procedures around containment, investigation, notification, remediation, and post-incident review for data breaches or near misses. Tabletop exercises evaluate response preparedness and coordination under time pressures, illuminating areas for enhancement. Lessons further improve maturity.

DATA GOVERNANCE

Compliance-centric data governance maps all data flows, conducts privacy impact assessments, and assigns ownership, retention, and destruction schedules for consistency according to purpose limitations, consent, and individual rights principles. Categorizations support applying controls and response priorities proportionately based on sensitivities.

METRICS AND OVERSIGHT

Regular governance, risk, and compliance reporting measures progress and document issues through metrics around training participation, testing results, policy acknowledgments, and incidents. Benchmarking security programs enhances preparations for identifying optimization areas. Oversight committees impartially direct continual improvement and hold organizations accountable for living the compliance culture.

THIRD-PARTY MANAGEMENT

Third parties entrusted with data require managing commensurate to risks and regulatory obligations. Vendor selection involves evaluating security and privacy controls while contractual terms clearly delineate third-party responsibilities for meeting compliance requirements. Ongoing assessments monitor partners' adherence and investigate deficiencies necessitating remediation. Data transfers undergo impact assessments and employ controls like anonymization and minimizing sensitivity. Upon termination, records undergo secure destruction according to retention schedules. Strict oversight maintains protections end-to-end.

INDIVIDUAL RIGHTS MANAGEMENT

Compliance cultivates respect for individual rights like access, correction, deletion, and data portability. Streamlined systems fulfill requests promptly according to jurisdiction-specific procedures and timeframes. Documented consent captures permission granularity through transparent communications, avoiding inadvertent over-collection. Continuous authentication prevents unauthorized access or amendment.

PRIVACY BY DESIGN

Forward-looking data minimization and privacy impact assessments facilitate building compliance into designs from project onsets. Architectures avoid unnecessary data uses and exposures by default through limited collection, strong authentication, and controls limiting scope creep over time according to need-to-know access principles. Preparations establish compliant foundations for future capabilities and growth.

COMPLIANCE AS A COMPETITIVE DIFFERENTIATOR

Proactive compliance strengthens security posture, operational resilience, and continuous process enhancement culture, enabling agility amid evolving regulatory landscapes. Robust programs evidence risk management integrity to partners and regulators, becoming reputational assets versus liabilities. Maturity benchmarking highlights progress in attracting client trust through responsible practices, keeping "access" in balance with "protection."

Security Auditing

Security auditing evaluates controls protecting sensitive systems and data through unbiased examination and testing. We will explore how planning, executing, and documenting thorough audits strengthen security postures while fulfilling regulatory evaluations. When conducted conscientiously according to professional standards, auditing improves protection maturity over time.

PLANNING THE AUDIT

Scoping defines auditable entities, timeframes, and objectives based on risks, requirements, and priorities. Resourcing involves designating an audit team with the requisite expertise, independence, and impartiality free from conflicts when assessing their own work. Notification prepares auditees while preliminary research collects policies, documentation, and prior findings.

PRE-ENGAGEMENT ACTIVITY

Baseline understanding involves exploring the audit site's technical and organizational security environments through documentation reviews and initial interviews. Control frameworks like NIST CSF help assess expected maturity levels. Sampling identifies test candidates according to risk significance while sensitizing staff maintains cooperative attitudes.

ON-SITE FIELDWORK

Methodical fieldwork tests control using inspection, observation, trace exercise, and reperformance considering documentation, systems, and personnel adherence. Interviews probe into procedures, exceptions, anomalies, or deficiencies, uncovering root causes. Documentation and forensic tools support investigative phases as needed.

CONTROL EVALUATION AND REPORTING

Findings undergo severity rating proportional to impact balancing vulnerabilities, likelihood, and mitigation costs. Prioritization considers remediation urgency and complexity. Draft reports undergo validation, protecting auditee rights before confidential distribution to oversight committees and regulators, as necessary. Action plans formalize remediation responsibilities, milestones, and assessments.

FOLLOW-UP ENGAGEMENT

Periodic follow-ups verify satisfactory or nearing completion remediation according to agreed-upon timelines and monitor control sustainability. Reporting highlights progress, residual risks, and lessons, strengthening long-term protections through continuous learning. Non-concurrence escalates to leadership according to materiality.

QUALITY ASSURANCE

Programs ensure consistent execution quality and impartiality, meeting professional standards. Peer reviews catch subjectivity while record-keeping meets. Traceability and supportability requirements. Regular competence development and certifications boost precision. User feedback identifies enhancements keeping pace with environments. Independence avoids complacency, risking integrity.

SELECTING AUDIT TYPES

Organizations employ different audit types appropriately based on functions, risks, schedules, and requirements. Regulatory assessments certify compliance, while independent third-party or internal audits provide an objective perspective. Technical audits examine infrastructure and configurations in-depth. Management system audits validate frameworks and governance structures.

PERSONNEL AUDITS

Routine personnel record reviews and background checks evaluate hiring screening effectiveness and identify risks from privileged users' access, credentials, or entitlements. Specialized digital forensics capabilities support investigating anomalous user activities or suspected security incidents involving employees or contractors. Findings merit remediation confidentiality according to severity.

EXTERNAL AUDITING CONSIDERATIONS

Third parties undergo vetting to ensure requisite skills, certifications, references, and standardized audit methodologies are executed impartially. Scope limitations address exposed IP risks, while confidentiality agreements govern the distribution of sensitive findings according to agreed reporting obligations. Contracts clarify deliverables, schedules, and liability avoidance, maintaining freedom of independent judgment.

METRICS AND MATURITY ASSESSMENT

Defining key performance indicators like findings closure rates, coverage, project timeliness, and client satisfaction benchmark quality and efficiency. Maturity models compare control implementations and response enhancements against targets identifying capability gaps requiring elevation. Benchmarking informs continuous evolution, aligning with advancing risks and standards.

REGULATORY EVALUATION COORDINATION

Many regulations, including industry certifications, data privacy laws, and security frameworks, necessitate audits demonstrating diligence. Collaboration streamlines redundant assessments, integrating objectives, samples, schedules, and report outputs across requirements. Coordination reduces disruptions while demonstrating comprehensive oversight.

Compliance Reporting and Documentation

Robust governance and auditing require comprehensive reporting to demonstrate diligence responsibly. We will discuss strategies for generating substantive compliance documentation and reports aligning security programs with evolving regulatory and industry obligations. Automation, templates, and analytics applied judiciously optimize workload and consistency over manual processes.

DEFINING REPORT TYPES

Objectives guide selecting routine, event-driven, and ad hoc report categories, including vulnerability assessments, audit findings, breach reports, risk profiles, remediation updates, training metrics, and management dashboards. Specialized reports fulfill program-specific mandates around frameworks, certifications, and contractual obligations.

DESIGNING TEMPLATES

Consistent, standardized templates organize report sections around purpose, background, methodology, key findings, priority rankings, timeline commitments, and sign-offs according to intended audiences and documentation requirements. Automated reporting tools incorporate templates while allowing customization flexibilities for edge cases or new directives over time.

COLLECTING SOURCE DATA

Harmonizing data sources like vulnerability scanning logs, audit work papers, remediation tracking data, training records, risk inventories, and incidents involving personally identifiable information requires systematic integration into reporting systems according to sensitive handling procedures and retention obligations.

QUALITY ASSURANCE

Defined review and approval workflows involving stakeholders to eliminate defects prior to distribution through cross-validation of results, recommendations, presentation quality, and regulatory conformance. Validation confirms accuracy, completeness, and readability, improving credibility. Versioning capabilities manage revisions transparently.

DISTRIBUTING REPORTS

Secure distribution methods involve internal portal access controls and encryption for confidential oversight committees, boards, and executives alongside customized external submissions according to appropriate contractual obligations, publication requirements, and victim notifications, preserving privacy. Delivery notifications maintain availability accountability and document handling standards.

ANALYTICS AND VISUALIZATION

Data-driven analytical dashboards and graphical representations contextualize volume metrics, trends, performance indicators, maturity benchmarks, and outlier findings, facilitating executive-level prioritization and resource allocation decisions. Visual abstraction harmonizes complexity succinctly for diverse audiences and communication channels according to specialized needs.

ARCHIVING AND RETENTION

Document lifecycle management according to legal hold and records retention specifications involves cataloging reports within centralized, compliant repositories according to confidentiality markings while applying consistent naming conventions and revision tracking. Retention schedules adhere to jurisdictional stipulations facilitating audits and reviews.

OPERATIONALIZING DOCUMENTATION

To facilitate routine documentation generation aligned with regulatory and industry benchmarking conventions, configuration management platforms integrate vulnerability scans, audit findings, remediation status feeds, metrics databases, and incidents into report production interfaces according to definable business logic and permissions. Automation streamlines documentation.

MATURITY ASSESSMENTS

Standardized frameworks evaluate governance, risk management, and compliance management program sophistication against maturity model levels. Benchmarking against peers and longitudinal trends identifies excellence while pinpointing areas requiring elevation to strengthen overall maturity, guiding focused improvement planning. Demonstrating enhancements strengthens posture.

REGULATORY FILINGS

Specialized submissions to regulators, clients, or industry consortiums focus on security incidents, breaches, auditing statements for certification renewal, notification supplements, and annual risk reporting requirements. Careful presentation aligns with mandated formatting, timing, and content instructions according to legal nuances for each.

INTERNATIONAL CONSIDERATIONS

Handling cross-border data transfers and localized documentation storage as per jurisdiction-specific privacy directives involves rigorously considering cultural sensitivities, language preferences, and legal variations. Harmonization facilitates coherent, globally compliant reporting practices. Independent auditing provides added reassurance.

SUCCESSION PLANNING

Onboarding documentation and knowledge transfers orient new hires on the value of diligent reporting frameworks supporting informed decision-making through familiarizing them with customized templates, technologies underpinning report generation, and records management procedures. Clear handoffs sustain competence.

BOOK 5
Leadership and Hands-On Exercises

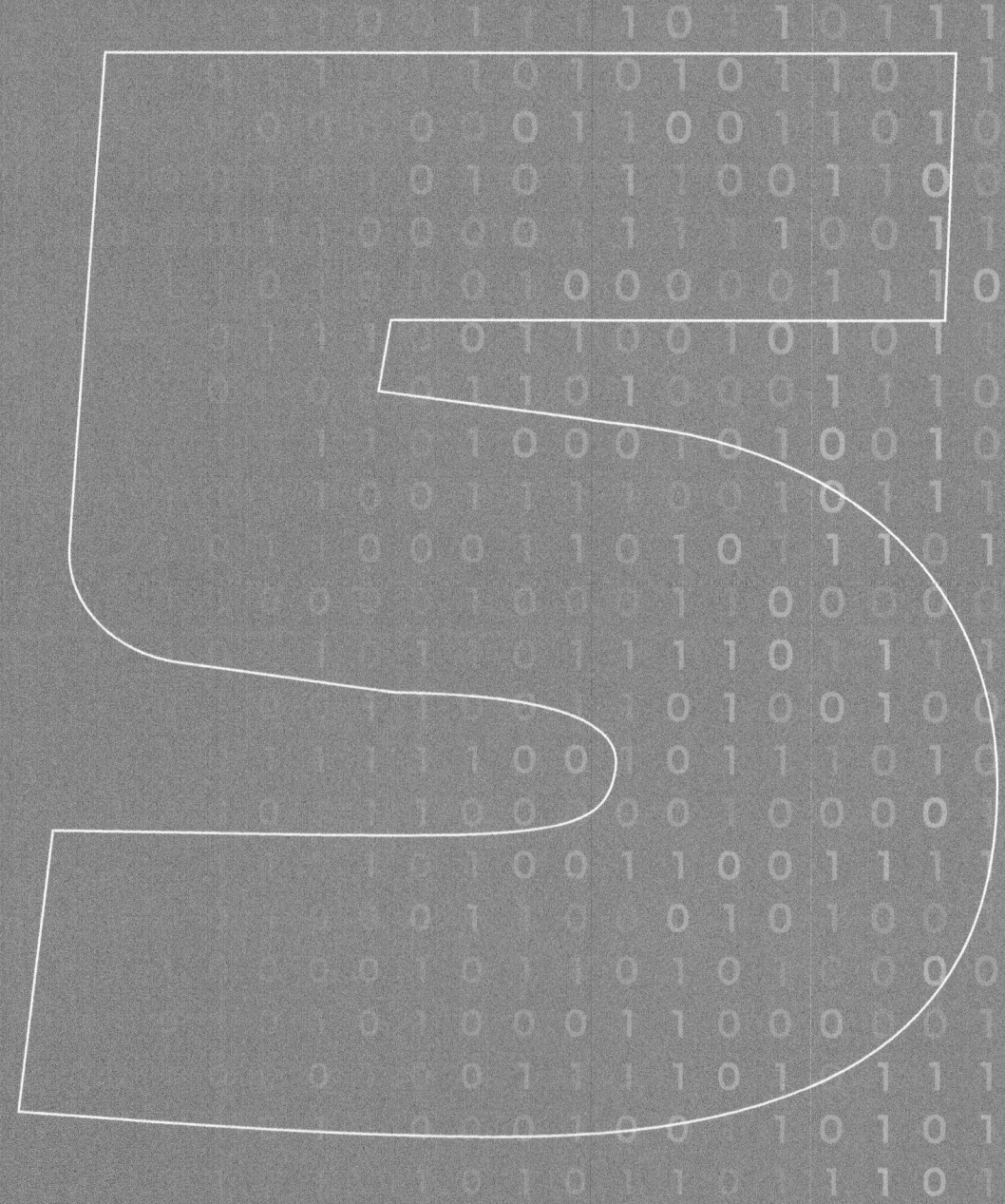

CHAPTER 17
Leading Your Security Team

Building a Security Team

As a new cybersecurity leader, building an effective security team is one of the most important responsibilities you will have. The team you assemble will directly impact your organization's ability to detect, prevent, and respond to cyber threats. In this chapter, we will explore the key considerations for recruiting and developing a high-performing security team.

ESTABLISHING SKILL REQUIREMENTS

The first step is to carefully define the skill set requirements for your team. You will need a mix of technical skills like networking, coding, and forensics, as well as soft skills like communication, critical thinking, and stakeholder management. Determine which roles are needed based on your organization's risk profile, compliance obligations, and security program maturity. Common roles include threat intelligence analysts, vulnerability managers, incident responders, security architects, and awareness specialists. Each role may require specific certifications or education levels, too. Having a clear understanding of your needs makes the hiring process more effective.

RECRUITING TEAM MEMBERS

With requirements defined, you can start recruiting candidates with the desired skill sets. Post job openings on security-focused job boards and sites geared toward military veterans transitioning to cyber roles. Leverage your professional network on LinkedIn to find potential candidates as well. Consider hosting an internship program to develop fresh talent. Review resumes thoroughly to identify the strongest candidates matching at least 70% of requirements. Conduct phone screens before moving qualified resumes forward to in-person interviews. Ask competency and scenario-based questions to truly evaluate skills. Background and reference checks are critical at the end of the process before making an offer.

DEVELOPING THROUGH TRAINING

No team starts fully formed, so establish a training and development budget. Ongoing learning is vital as threats evolve rapidly. Prioritize foundation-level certifications for all members within the first year. More senior team members can pursue advanced technical certifications or executive leadership tracks. Leverage free resources from SANS, ISC2, and the FBI whenever possible. Schedule regular internal seminars where members share newly learned skills with each other. Recommended skills to focus on include threat hunting, forensics, coding, and compliance frameworks like NIST CSF or ISO 27001. With supportive development opportunities, your team will stay motivated and constantly improve over time.

FOSTERING THE RIGHT CULTURE

Beyond skills, you must create a high-functioning team culture. From onboarding, emphasize the importance of open communication, cooperation, and mutual respect. Lead from the front by exemplifying these cultural attributes yourself. Encourage collaboration over territorialism between teams focused on different controls like identity, network, or application security. Implement ways for members to provide anonymous feedback to identify issues promptly. Also, have fun together through morale-building social activities outside work. With the right culture, team dynamics and morale remain strong as the industry and threats change.

PERFORMANCE MANAGEMENT

Implementing clear performance expectations and consistent reviews helps individuals and the team progress together toward goals. Define objectives for each role based on their function and experience level. Ensure they are specific, measurable progress markers. Check in frequently on ongoing work through one-on-one standups in addition to quarterly reviews. Recognize accomplishments publicly and provide constructive private feedback to reinforce strengths and address weaknesses. Address underperformance through documented coaching plans before termination becomes necessary. Reward high performers with bonuses, promotions, and other meaningful incentives to retain top talent.

KEEPING THE TEAM SECURE

As the leader responsible for your organization's security, you must lead by example and role model best practices for your own team as well. Enforce strict access controls and require regular cybersecurity awareness refresher training, even for technical experts. Monitor accounts for anomalies and require long, unique passwords to be changed frequently. Conduct periodic security audits of team members' systems and code. Most importantly, maintain open communication so they feel comfortable reporting any suspected issues promptly. A breach resulting from a team member's own system exposes the entire program. Taking proactive steps protects both your agency and the livelihoods of the team.

MANAGING THE TEAM

In addition to establishing roles and guiding development, an effective leader manages day-to-day team operations. This involves:

Workload Distribution

When projects and incident response tasks arise, the leader ensures work is distributed fairly according to skills and availability. Overloading certain members while others are idle breeds frustration. Consider factors like deadlines, complexity levels, and individual strengths when delegating.

Communications

Frequent communication keeps the remote and in-office teams aligned. Daily stand-ups track progress while also surfacing blockers. A group messaging channel shares updates promptly. 1:1 check-ins address any private concerns. Monthly all-hands meetings review goals and metrics with the entire program.

Governance and Guidance

Establish change management and documentation standards. Formal review processes validate work quality. Technical guidance centralizes knowledge and avoids redundant work. Governance helps comply with frameworks while also instilling discipline, which is important for success.

Mentorship

Pair less experienced members with senior team members as mentors. Schedule mentorship sessions to transfer knowledge more effectively than occasional questions. Mentors assist with career development and guidance on important soft skills.

Work-Life Balance

Long hours handling constant crises can burn team members out quickly. Encourage using available vacation time. Flexible schedules accommodate personal needs when possible. Promote mental health resources to manage the stresses of the job.

Budgeting and Purchases

Project and operating budgets must cover tools, training, and other needs. The leader evaluates proposals and justifies requests. Purchase processes happen efficiently with guidance on business requirements and procurement policies.

Crisis Management

The leader remains calm under pressure to direct immediate incident response activities. Delegate research and mitigation tasks clearly. Post-incident reviews identify lessons to refine procedures for the next crisis.

Encouraging Growth Beyond Routine Tasks

The most motivated team members want growth opportunities. Sponsor their participation in industry groups and conferences. Rotations into partner security teams broaden perspectives on differing program approaches. Promotions and expanded responsibilities retain top performers for the long term.

Leadership in Cybersecurity

Taking on a leadership role in cybersecurity involves unique challenges and responsibilities. Beyond technical knowledge, strong leadership skills are required to drive strategic initiatives, cultivate collaboration across business units, and advocate for the security program. We will discuss key aspects of leadership in cybersecurity and best practices for success in this critical role.

ESTABLISHING VISION AND GOALS

One of the primary duties of any leader is setting the strategic vision and defining goals that align with the organization's broader objectives. In cybersecurity, this requires a deep understanding of emerging threats, regulatory landscapes, and technological capabilities. Leaders must collaborate internally to establish realistic yet ambitious goals that strengthen security posture over 1-3 year horizons. Goals should be specific, measurable, and supported by defined initiatives and budgets. Clearly communicating this roadmap inspires teams and gains support from senior stakeholders.

GAINING INTERNAL INFLUENCE

To be effective, cyber leaders must be a trusted voice that influences decision-making across the organization. This involves active relationship building and compromise over mandates. Leaders serve as security advisors, highlighting risks and compliance obligations but also viable solution options. Compelling data and stories convince others that security enables business objectives. Leaders also serve as role models, establishing a "tone from the top" through diligent personal security practices. Earning influence takes consistency over time to counter perceptions of security as a business inhibitor.

COMPLIANCE AND GOVERNANCE

Security frameworks like NIST CSF provide structure, but successful programs require customizing controls to the unique business environment. Leaders must understand how compliance demands integrate with routine operations for sustainable success over audits. Governance works best enabled through education versus enforced alone through policy. Leaders coach others to make prudent security choices integral to their jobs versus an "add-on." This engagement prevents controls from becoming disassociated from real risks over time.

LEADING THROUGH ADVERSITY

Despite best efforts, breaches and failures do occur, requiring rapid, high-pressure responses. Composed leaders make tough decisions objectively while supporting shaken teams. Transparency with regulators and the public reassures stakeholders in resolving crises promptly. Unbiased post-mortems identify true root causes, limiting "blame games" that damage credibility. Adversity often strengthens legitimate programs by revealing priorities and gaps for agile improvements. Resilient leaders turn failures into renewed motivation by recasting them as learning opportunities.

BUILDING TALENT AND SUCCESSION

To advance beyond routine "firefighting," leaders must develop technical and strategic skills across expanding teams. Formal training coupled with mentoring, rotations, and conferences cultivate a vibrant in-house talent pool and ensure knowledge continuity amid inevitable turnover. Leaders clarify expectations and recognize strengths for promotions to retain and attract top performers in a competitive field. Succession planning prepares qualified successors and allows experienced leaders to take on advisory roles for ongoing guidance.

DEVELOPING STRATEGIC PARTNERSHIPS

No single security team can go it alone - forging strategic partnerships amplifies capabilities and knowledge. Leaders participate in industry organizations and initiatives to advocate for issues and benchmark continuously. Relations with cyber insurers, technology vendors, and managed service providers open doors to novel offerings and support. Law enforcement collaborations safeguard the organization and community in times of crisis. Academia partnerships seed the next-generation technical workforce through research and internships. Strategic networking remains vital to any mature program.

MANAGING PROJECTS AND BUDGETS

Effective project and budget management are essential responsibilities for any security leader. Some key aspects include:

Defining Project Scope

The leader works with teams to clearly define the requirements, deliverables, timelines, and success metrics for each security project. A well-defined scope prevents scope creep and ensures projects satisfy intended objectives.

Developing Detailed Plans

Project plans outline tasks, dependencies, resource requirements, and timelines. The leader reviews plans to confirm feasibility and raise potential issues proactively. The plan serves as a baseline to measure progress.

Budget Planning and Requests

Expansive needs often outstrip available funds, so the leader prioritizes based on organizational risk appetite and compliance mandates. Well-reasoned budget requests supported by documented needs are more likely to gain approval.

Procurement Process Management

The leader shepherds procurement processes for tools, services, and technology. This involves developing RFPs, evaluating vendor proposals, contract negotiations, purchase approvals, and invoice tracking. Efficiency saves money and prevents project delays.

Status Tracking and Reporting

Frequent check-ins keep projects on track through a review of task status, metrics, and emerging issues. The leader consolidates status across all projects for regular reporting to senior leaders and stakeholders.

Change Management

Scope or timeline adjustments may be needed as projects progress. The leader evaluates change requests through a formal review process, balancing priorities with potential impacts and ensuring concessions remain valid and approved.

Issue Escalation and Resolution

Project blockers beyond a manager's control require timely escalation. The leader's authority and influence facilitate resolving dependencies and allocating resources to remove barriers impacting schedules and budgets.

Post-Project Reviews

Lessons learned through comprehensive post-mortems improve future efforts. The leader integrates feedback to update policies, refine cost estimates, and highlight what went well for replication on later initiatives.

Continuous Improvements

Insights enable the leader to mature processes continuously, adopting industry and project management best practices suited to the organizational culture and risks. This progress drives overall program optimization.

Managing Security Projects

Managing cybersecurity projects effectively is paramount as threats evolve rapidly and budgets remain constrained. While technical skills are important, strong leadership through planning, communication, and process maturity is what drives consistency and success over time. As leaders, we must consider the diverse needs of all stakeholders. Projects aim to reduce risk but also enable business objectives and compliance. Achieving buy-in requires understanding differing perspectives and balancing priorities. Comprehensive scoping lays this foundation by outlining objectives through collaboration. Leading complex initiatives is challenging yet rewarding work. We are entrusted to oversee initiatives critical to the organization's protection. There is no room for error, given the stakes. Our roles, therefore, demand diligence, transparency, and skillful problem-solving to consistently hit objectives on schedule and budget.

DEFINING PROJECT SCOPE

Thorough scoping involves engaging subject matter experts and targeting users or teams early. This ensures realistic expectations around requirements that can truly reduce vulnerabilities or streamline processes as intended. Overpromising typically leads to later issues. We must also consider how the project integrates with existing security controls and programs to optimize investments. Duplication wastes funds, while gaps in coordination can undermine results. Knowledge transfer plans should be outlined as well to facilitate adoption and support post-deployment. Key risks and potential mitigating plans should be identified during initial discussions. This allows proactively addressing obstacles rather than reactionary firefighting. Dependencies on other teams or upcoming organizational changes need accounting, too. Finally, success criteria should be specific and measurable to permit objective evaluation later.

DEVELOPING COMPREHENSIVE PLANS

Developing detailed plans involves breaking down scoped requirements into actionable tasks with reasonable time estimates. Leaders provide expertise toward estimating complexity to avoid overconfidence biases. Logical dependencies between tasks should drive sequenced planning. Resource requirements must be thoroughly understood whether software, hardware, staffing needs, or specialized skills. This enables realistic budgeting. Subject matter experts should validate whether necessary domain knowledge will be accessible. Potential issues and contingencies also warrant consideration at the planning stage. Change management procedures, clear communication strategies, and escalation paths to promote controlled pivot points if needed. Periodic milestone reviews keep distributed teams synchronized as plans evolve. Plans set the baseline, so they must receive rigorous yet expeditious stakeholder review and refinement before finalization. This collaborative process strengthens plans to set the project up for controlled execution and success. With strong plans, predictability and accountability improve significantly.

CHAPTER 18
Incident Response and Recovery

Incident Handling Procedures

Despite best prevention efforts, security incidents will occur and must be addressed promptly to minimize damage. Developing standardized yet flexible procedures guides teams through a process ensuring comprehensive responses. As the leader, defining and socializing these procedures is paramount for organizational readiness.

ESTABLISHING CLEAR ROLES AND RESPONSIBILITIES

Responsible parties, from incident handlers to forensic analysts to public relations, must be unambiguously designated. Leadership clearly communicates expectations, from after-hours contact protocols to evidence-handling procedures. Accountability reduces delays while duties leverage in-house expertise. Regular reviews address personnel changes.

TRAINING AND EXERCISING THE PLAN

Procedures exist on paper without validation through training. Leadership schedules classroom sessions and realistic simulations annually at a minimum. Exercises uncover gaps remedied before crises, build cohesion under pressure, and fulfill compliance obligations. Scenario variation develops broad skills across likely and extreme situations.

DETECTION AND INITIAL RESPONSE

24/7 monitoring and routine testing/verification ensure alerts reflect actual incidents versus false positives. On-call staff receive alerts empowering rapid containment limiting the scope. Preliminary evidence collected according to standard operating procedures maintains the chain of custody. Impact assessments direct priority levels for mobilization.

INVESTIGATION AND ANALYSIS

Cross-functional teams conduct contextual analysis to improve understanding of individual facets. Timelines impacted assets, and initial next steps emerge from gathering all insights. Prior incidents inform hypotheses tested through comprehensive hunting. Careful documentation forms official records vetted by oversight.

REMEDIATION, RECOVERY, AND COMMUNICATION

Lessons instill continuous defensive enhancements while direct remediation resolves vulnerabilities exploited. Recovery restores normal operations validated through testing. Clear, factual statements balance transparency with sensitivity. Updates track progress rebuilding confidence. Post-incident reviews institute permanent improvements sustaining readiness.

POLICY, REGULATION, AND LESSONS LEARNED

Anonymous aggregation and high-level documentation protect privacy while satisfying mandatory breach reporting and audits. Actionably disseminating findings through briefings and updated procedures stimulates cultural shift. Key performance indicators track progress maturing process effectiveness and compliance over time.

EXERCISING CONTINUOUS IMPROVEMENT

Emerging threats and technologies, along with changing risk landscapes, necessitate dynamic procedures. Leaders champion benchmarking successes, considering staff and regulatory feedback, and automating manual tasks. Refinement sustains agility, assuring comprehensive yet efficient incident management as needs evolve.

DETECTING AND RESPONDING TO INCIDENTS

Once procedures are established, effective detection and initial response are crucial. Some important considerations include:

Monitoring and Alerting

Comprehensive monitoring of networks, endpoints, applications, and logs ensures threats are detected promptly. Well-configured security tools minimize false positives to avoid alert fatigue.

On-Call Rotation

A cycle of trained personnel is available after hours and on weekends to triage alerts. Rapid acknowledgment calms organizations during off-hours incidents.

Initial Assessment and Containment

First responders quickly assess the scope, vector, and potential business impact. Prioritized containment actions like account lockouts limit ongoing damage.

Evidence Preservation

Strict chain of custody procedures when collecting memory images, logs, and other artifacts ensure evidentiary integrity, which is important for attribution and prosecution.

Communications and Mobilization

Additional teams are notified according to incident severity for engagement of relevant disciplines like forensics, crisis management, and legal.

Reporting and Notifications

Upstream stakeholders and any regulators or law enforcement are promptly alerted according to breach notification policies and laws.

Emergency Response Procedures

For critical incidents, disaster recovery and business continuity plans are activated to maintain core business functions and communications.

Lessons Learned Integration

Observations from each incident response further refine processes and controls, reducing future impact and response times through experience.

Exercising and Improvement

Regular drills keep skills sharp and reveal gaps to shore up before real crises. After-action reviews identify strengths as well as areas for enhancement.

With detection, containment, communication, and iterative improvement prioritized, organizations can minimize harm from inevitable security events.

Forensics and Investigation

Forensic investigations seek to thoroughly understand security incidents and extract valuable lessons. As security leaders, we must oversee procedures to ensure high-quality results through standardized yet adaptive approaches. This process, though demanding, strengthens defenses by providing crucial insights into remediation, attribution, and prevention for the future.

PLANNING AND PREPARATION

Readying skilled responders involves comprehensive planning. Response plans cover common evidence types and necessary tools across networks, endpoints, servers, and mobile devices. On-call rotations maintain coverage while outside experts expand capacity. Regular training tests plan feasibility and cover new collection methods. Digital forensics also requires dedicated, secured workspaces with appropriate hardware and software setups validated through checks. Proper training establishes skills and prepares documentation workflows to streamline real investigations.

EVIDENCE IDENTIFICATION, PRESERVATION, AND DOCUMENTATION

The response begins by identifying types of relevant evidence. Targeted collections focus efforts, avoiding non-pertinent data overwhelming analysts. Strict chain of custody procedures covering documentation and storage maintain legal defensibility if needed. Such safeguards guide all evidence handling by response teams from collection at endpoints through final preservation and analysis. Formally logged actions build meticulous records establishing the investigation's credibility.

LIVE RESPONSE AND MEMORY FORENSICS

When possible, promptly on-site live responses leverage unique privileges. Experts directly monitor compromised hosts, pinpointing active malicious processes, open connections, and concealed files otherwise inaccessible. Volatile memory imaging captures intrinsic runtime details before system disruption clears prints. Given fleeting windows, finely tuned standard operating procedures facilitate live response coordination under pressure.

NON-VOLATILE DATA ACQUISITION AND EXAMINATION

Imaging entire disks, volumes, or files creates self-contained snapshots, enabling safe offline examination without risking modification. Smaller targeted information pulls like specific directories or registry keys suffice in many cases. Regardless, hashing confirms that copied contents mirror originals without data corruption during transfer or storage. Configuration management then safeguards master evidence.

EVIDENCE PROCESSING AND INVESTIGATION

Processing tools extract evidenced data from unusable formats into searchable forms assessed by a range of specialized forensic analysis utilities. Together, these facilitate chronology reconstruction and reveal artifacts shedding light on attack vectors, lateral movement, exfiltrated information, and more. Forensic analysts methodically explore all leads according to documented review procedures.

REPORTING AND CONTINUOUS IMPROVEMENT

Conclusions undergo peer scrutiny before reporting summarizes findings and recommendations. Documentation standards produce structured, defensible reports. Lessons from each investigation enhance readiness through process, tool, or training updates identified in reviews. Proactive research stays abreast of new collection techniques and analysis methodologies against emerging threats. Together, refinement and adaptation strengthen the program in the long term. As leaders, diligently overseeing planning, training, evidence handling, and peer reviews help uncover the truth while promoting operational improvements. Thorough yet efficient investigations empower remediation and prevention.

Business Continuity and Disaster Recovery

As threats evolve, maintaining continuity grows more complex yet critical. Leaders spearhead rigorous yet flexible plans, empowering resilience against diverse risks. Comprehensiveness considers technical, physical, and human factors; agility addresses continual changes. Regular validation strengthens readiness for supporting missions despite disruption.

IMPACT ASSESSMENTS AND PRIORITIZATION

Assessments identify single points of failure and cascade impacts. Granular data from departments informs tolerable outages to prioritize recovery. Threat modeling assesses geographic, infrastructure, and vendor risks. Testing exercises verify assessments' accuracy, guiding strategic choices. Prioritization directly links to organizational priorities and obligations. Assessments analyze interdependencies across divisions to recognize secondary and tertiary consequences. Bottom-up data collection involves subject matter experts understanding intricacies. Threat modeling incorporates future growth projections and changing environmental factors like climate risks or political instability. Contextual data informs likelihood and impacts. Validation testing put the organization under simulated outages gauging tolerance.

RECOVERY STRATEGIES

Leaders validate the technical and financial feasibility of options like redundant infrastructure, portable devices, work area recovery, and alternate facilities. Strategies balance continuity needs against the budget while incorporating customizable elements. Documentation standards produce actionable checklists for systematic changeovers. Regular reviews address shifting technologies and risks. Cost-benefit analyses ascertain the value of mitigation investments. Sensitivity testing evaluates adequacy under various incidents. Strategies incorporate flexibility for inevitable changes unforeseen presently. Modular elements accommodate growth while limiting waste. Customizations allow adaptations reflecting departmental or geographic nuances. Standardization streamlines coordination where sensible.

EMERGENCY RESPONSE PROCEDURES

Crisis management and communication plans with clear escalation paths expedite assistance. External partnerships pre-agree surge support terms. Procedures outline interfaces to public resources considering varying localized hazards. Socialization builds understanding for smooth coordination under pressure. Response tiers establish handoff criteria from containing minor incidents to declaring disasters. Escalation considers impacts, size, and urgencies. Communication protocols cover accessing populations across digital and traditional means. Notifications balance timeliness with avoiding panic. Socialization involves simulated exercises and reference materials for embedding processes into the staff psyche beyond the paper plan. Training accommodates ebbing tenures. Oversight validates comprehension, resources, and agreements to remain current. Subject matter experts ensure procedures account for the latest technological and regulatory changes.

ACTIVATION AND RECOVERY OPERATIONS

Drills rehearse scenarios from detection through executing recovery actions. Playbooks guide reversing firewalls, cutting over DNS and client notifications for minimal disruptions. Recovery sites undergo regular data synchronization and migration testing with pass/fail criteria. Learning objectives drive after-action reviews and process refinements. Drills validate inter-team coordination effectiveness, testing communication channels and off-hours support. Observed participation corroborates comprehension. Testing encompasses various activation timeframes and staffing availability scenarios. Parameters incorporate surprises to establish adaptability. Pass/fail criteria establish objectivity. Learning objectives focus on critiques constructively. Documentation provides governance and accountability.

INFRASTRUCTURE AND ENVIRONMENTAL MONITORING

Redundant monitoring platforms alert on-premises failures from connectivity issues to HVAC/power abnormalities. Policies mandate notification timeframes from vendors, facilitating rapid remediation. Dependable geo-diverse systems balance reliability with connectivity. Strategies to counter supply chain issues impacting component access. Platforms integrate various sensor types, from security to building management systems. Artificial intelligence analyzes for interdependencies and subtle anomalies. Policies cover various severity levels, from informational to activating formal responses. Escalation considers impacts and a window for containment. Agreements outline service-level objectives for uptime, change management communications, and problem-resolution tenures. Contracts incorporate flexibility for inevitable evolution.

CRITICAL DATA PROTECTION

Standard backups, retention periods, and immutable offsite storage safeguard against data loss. Test restoration ensures the recovery of data and applications. Encryption and segmented access controls maintain sensitive data confidentiality throughout recovery activations. Backup media undergo routine integrity verification and refreshment. Offsite arrangements balance accessibility, security, and connectivity. Testing incorporates failure simulations and time boxing to establish production readiness. Recovery point/time objectives are validated through timing. Key management and access controls incorporate segregation of duties for oversight. Encryption uses vetted algorithms impervious to future cracking.

TEAM PREPAREDNESS

Cross-training bolsters redundancy, while succession planning mitigates single points of failure among personnel. Simulation participation verifies understanding and skills. Mental health resources support wellbeing under pressure. Training budgets accommodate evolving best practices for sustaining expertise. Succession maps recognize backups for each duty. Documentation provides institutional memory outweighing individuals. Simulation design incorporates various stressors, from data loss to injuries. Realism tests adaptability and stamina. Wellness programs address inherent burnout risks. Education cultivates resilience, acknowledging impacts' longevity. Support normalizes struggles, empowering optimization.

Tuition and certifications allocate funds annually. Benchmarking transfers innovations before they become outdated. Partnerships supply surplus training amid deficiencies.

CONTINUOUS IMPROVEMENT

Incident reviews identify enhancements across technical, process, and social aspects. Benchmarking against frameworks and industry peers drives progress in maturing resilience. Program oversight strengthens organizational mission assurance despite uncertain conditions. After actions incorporate multi-perspective interviews beyond direct perceptions. Documentation provides traceability and discernment of recurring weaknesses. Framework benchmarking establishes maturity positioning, while case studies provide leading practices. Collaboration transfers viable optimizations. Program steering committees include executive sponsors and multi-disciplinary advisors. Partnership maintains the balance of perspectives beyond individual silos or tenures. Advocacy cultivates recognition of investments safeguarding mission-critical operations countering competing priorities. Signaling prioritization bolsters sustainment.

CHAPTER 19
Security Culture and Awareness Programs

Creating a Security Culture

Cultivating security awareness necessitates patience and persistence over unilateral mandates. The change stems from understanding rather than fear of punishment. Open communication helps employees internalize the importance of their roles versus reacting to external controls. Leaders establish approachability to address concerns promptly. Approachability and transparency build buy-in for new policies or tools. Further, recognizing exemplary security behaviors amongst ranks inspires others through their example. A balance of education, empathy, and accountability suits diverse personalities and positions within the organization. Not all learn identically, so diversifying training caters to different strengths and backgrounds.

COMMUNICATIONS AND TRAINING

Introducing security awareness as an enabling benefit rather than a hindrance fosters receptiveness. Demonstrating relevance to job functions through examples cultivates ownership of lessons. Development opportunities like certifications and skill shares further cement retention by rewarding mastery. Internally recognized credentials signal leadership investment in careers. Individualizing learning paths allows for focusing on personal strengths. Department-specific content localizes global issues. Supplementary material keeps topics lively through current events. Testing facilitates a self-paced review of retained knowledge. Management participation in training signals priorities. Soliciting feedback also improves relevancy and delivery over time. Leveraging employee expertise produces peer-led sessions where comfortable. This involvement nurtures security champions.

DATA STEWARDSHIP AND HANDLING

Detailed education stresses protecting personally identifiable health information entrusted to employees through their roles. Sensitive data loss severely damages reputation and trust regardless of root causes. Proactively, classes highlight "insider risk" scenarios to internalize potential harm beyond technical controls. Personal accountability becomes prioritized over temporary non-compliance. Documentation standards for records retention minimize unnecessary file retention. Awareness around disposal protects disposed of hardware and papers. Oversight ensures protocols follow regulatory obligations. Acceptable use policies balance productivity and privacy. Technical controls alone cannot replace judgment. Resources provide guidance in navigating gray areas such as BYOD or remote work scenarios. Data governance initiatives bring together cross-functional leaders, validating policies that reflect operational realities. Feedback continually modernizes guidelines considering business model evolution. Committees vet third parties handling data on the organization's behalf.

USER-FOCUSED SECURITY

Ensuring a positive user experience with security tools is paramount. Early testing involves end users evaluating designs. Their feedback shapes configurations optimized for usability without compromising protections. Contextual information helps employees understand why certain tools are required, avoiding potential resentment over added steps like multifactor authentication. Leadership explains how user-centric designs ultimately benefit work by mitigating interruptions from incidents. Onboarding guides introduce all features at a user's own pace. Support hotlines and self-help resources provide assistance in resolving common issues independently. Recognizing employee expertise fosters internal "super users" who can then assist peers. Gamification advances some training by rewarding the completion of skill-building modules with virtual rewards and recognition. Targeting both novice and proficient users, varied content keeps enrichment engaging long-term. Accessibility evaluations consider varied learning styles and physical/cognitive abilities.

INTERNAL REPORTING

To cultivate open reporting of even minor issues, leadership emphasizes remediating vulnerabilities over punishment for unintended mistakes or oversight. Retrospective analyses focus on systemic enhancements versus individual blame. Anonymous incident submission forms allow raising concerns privately to address sensitivities. Additional options like encrypted internal hotlines provide alternatives for those uncomfortable directly engaging leadership. Reward programs recognize valued internal reporting that prompts helpful investigations. Publicly celebrating anonymous reports (without revealing identities) also incentivizes others to come forward by social proof. Whistleblower policies outline protections and processes for escalating legally mandated concerns externally, if necessary, as a last resort. However, fostering resolution from within strengthens shared responsibility over regulatory involvement whenever possible.

Security Awareness Training Programs

Leaders set the tone driving programs as a strategic security control versus checkbox obligation. Communicating importance garners support critical for long-term culture change. Training objectives directly align with organizational missions, values, and partnerships. Tying initiatives to measurable business outcomes like reduced losses demonstrates tangible value beyond perceptions. Metrics highlight the impact on revenues, productivity, and customer trust. Benchmarking adoption rates against frameworks evaluate positioning competitively.

NEEDS ASSESSMENT

Comprehensive assessment approaches involve quantitative and qualitative data. Metrics provide high-level trend analysis, while open-ended surveys capture nuanced views. Threat modeling incorporates external intelligence from intelligence communities and cybersecurity research partners. Insider perspectives balance strategic foresight. Assessment outcomes directly inform strategic plans outlining multi-year roadmaps. Objectives, KPIs, budget allocations, and resource requirements achieve long-range visions. The process involves cross-divisional representation to gain holistic organizational understanding. Frontline staff provide ground truth, complementing leadership perspectives. External benchmarking against industry peers broadens considerations beyond isolated data. Case studies offer additional reference points for interpreted needs.

CURRICULUM DESIGN

Modular design allows customization and just-in-time learning. Micro-modules suit momentary refresher needs. Content originating from diverse, credible sources—such as third-party research partnerships—enhances reliability. Case studies rooted in organizational or sector-specific events foster relevance. Learning tracks categorize proficiency levels from awareness to mastery certifications. Progressive learning accommodates varied paces. Multiple languages reach cultural diversity within global organizations to optimize comprehension. Closed captioning and audio transcripts make content accessible. Instructional design experts validate course architecture and activities stimulate critical thinking. Formative assessments provide coaches for skill-building.

AWARENESS EXERCISES

Exercise types involve technical and non-technical situations. Authentic scenarios target failures observed across different employee roles. Phishing simulations deliver a variety of lures imitating vectors like invoices or password resets. Advanced social engineering gauges persistent manipulation vulnerabilities. Tabletop exercises leverage different mediums—like role-playing simulations or live facilitated discussions. Walkthroughs reinforce documented incident response plans. Exercises are administered across varied time intervals to maintain engagement. Time-pressured deadlines mimic realistic pressures. Repeated tests track retention over weeks/months. Pre-briefs establish ground rules and objectives promoting psychological safety. Experts facilitate discussions preventing negative impacts. Debrief feedback follows structured discussions focusing on takeaways applicable to different functions. Reflections avoid personal critiques, improving openness.

COMMUNICATIONS AND RESOURCES

Dynamic resources meet users wherever work happens through a variety of accessible channels. Customizable subscription preferences tailor content types and frequency. Interactive training modules reinforce two-way engagement beyond passive information dissemination. Multimedia incorporates visualization, audio narration, and gamification components. Online curricula feature just-in-time microlearning and refresher modules with credentialing options. Self-paced exploration cultivates self-motivated mastery. Knowledge bases compile centralized FAQs and directives indexed for easy searching. Multilingual support promotes comprehension. Company intranets house awareness hub pages consolidating programs, resources, and community forums. Mobile optimization facilitates on-the-go access.

CONTINUOUS IMPROVEMENT

Process and outcome evaluations keep programs aligned with evolving business objectives, risk profiles, and technologies. Gap analyses uncover coverage areas demanding fresh focus. Independent third-party reviews supplement internal assessments with impartial perspectives on maturity. Recommendations strengthen credibility for skeptics. Usage and competency analytics measure impact beyond compliance metrics like completions. Surveys gauge sentiment shifts over time and adoption barriers. Benchmarking against industry frameworks and competitors assesses positioning for improvement. Case studies identify transferable strategies. After action reviews, dissect exercise takeaways frankly without individual blame. Findings directly update procedures, tools, and curricula. Leadership oversees program governance, resources, and executive sponsorship. Roadmaps coordinate multi-year development toward strategic visions.

Measuring the Effectiveness of Awareness Initiatives

Maximizing awareness requires proving efficacy through objective measurements. Leaders institute rigorous yet pragmatic assessment balancing needs. Outcome indicators complement activity tracking, illuminating initiatives' true influence. Benchmarking elevates practices through cross-functional partnerships and peer reviews. Together, measurements ensure relevance against objectives over time.

DEFINING OBJECTIVES

Objectives align with strategic plans and risk assessments. Qualitative and quantitative targets focus effort on priorities. Metrics prioritization considers feasibility. Reviews maintain agility against changes. Objectives undergo stakeholder consultation to ensure comprehension and buy-in. Operationalizing objectives into action plans mitigates subjectivities. Prioritization factors include return on investment, feasibility, regulations, and emerging threats against available budgets, tools, and expertise over timelines. Sensitivity analyses determine critical objectives under constraints.

Documentation standards produce version-controlled objective registers managed through change. Configuration management safeguards alignments. Review processes gather multi-departmental commentary on evolving realities, prompting objective reconsiderations.

CHOOSING METRICS

Indicators incorporate appropriate lagging and leading metrics. Surveys measure awareness and perception changes. Assessments gauge skills and retained knowledge. Analytical tools capture exercise participation and risk behavior alterations. Metric propriety factors in operationalization feasibility, reliability, validity, timeliness, and cost against value. Pragmatism balances granularity. Semantic differences require clarification. Instrumentation plans govern collection methods, timing, sampling strategies, integration with existing tools, and safeguarding privacy compliant with regulations. Piloting validates metrics, reflecting objectives, and prioritizing efforts accurately. Revisions incorporate feedback. Version control maintains a master metric set.

DATA COLLECTION

Protocols govern collection methods, tools, record-keeping, and change management. Instrumentation safeguards privacy and integrity. Baselines facilitate before-after comparisons. Third-party validation supplements internal data. Sampling frameworks generalize findings cost-effectively across populations too large, surveying entirely. Stratification enhances segmentation analyses. Consent processes respect ethical considerations. Transparency builds trust, encouraging honesty. Incentivization boosts voluntary participation. Third-party access follows agreements extending perspectives. Connections broaden datasets beyond isolated views. Robustness validates potential response biases. Change management oversees updates upon infrastructure or regulatory changes, ensuring continuity. Rigorous procedures cement reliability.

ANALYZING RESULTS

Data undergoes rigorous quantitative and qualitative analyses to validate trends. Segmentation reveals differences. Statistical significance testing attributes correlations. Gap assessments identify underperforming areas. Segmentation breaks down aggregations to explore demographic or operational differences within populations. Filtering isolates impactful factors. Gap assessments evaluate underperforming metrics and their root causes to prioritize remedies. Deterministic approaches exclude alternatives. Predictive modeling extrapolates likely future performance based on current trajectories and potential changes. Sensitivity analyses estimate variations' impact.

Triangulation validates findings through cross-verification between methodologies like qualitative and quantitative convergence. External review strengthens validity claims.

COMMUNICATING INSIGHTS

Structured reporting synthesizes findings and actionable recommendations. Visual dashboards convey trends transparently. Communication methods match stakeholder needs. Recognizing successes inspires continued participation. Reports adopt storytelling techniques that correlate analyses back to objectives clearly. Summaries accompany full versions. Visualizations convert complex data into understandable dashboards optimized for quick decision-making. Tailored communication considers diverse stakeholder types - from executives to frontline staff. Methods may include paper, digital, and presentation, depending on preferences and responsibilities. Accessibility standards apply. Progress highlights recognize top performers driving positive reinforcements. Stories feature improvements attributed to programs strengthening motivations. Events celebrate achievements fostering community.

REVIEW AND IMPROVEMENT

Initiatives undergo iterative optimization accounting for evaluation outputs and environmental changes. Adjustments balance improvements against introducing disruption. Documentation preserves institutional knowledge. The process involves multi-stakeholder consultation respecting varied viewpoints. Risk-based prioritization directs efforts proportionately. Change management oversees socializing, training, and cultural readiness. Documentation standards convert lessons into institutional memory that is resilient to staff changes. Guidelines govern updates referencing version histories. Configuration management safeguards master sources. Benchmarking identifies transferable practices supplementing internal perspectives. Case studies contextualize optimizations suitable within capacities. Experimentation cultivates innovation. Flexibility maintains agility, adjusting in a timely manner in reaction to disruptions while preserving momentum.

BENCHMARKING AND VALIDATION

Programs assess standings competitively while identifying strengths. Partnerships broaden considerations. Independent reviews provide impartial expertise, strengthening credibility. Oversight ensures rigor in aligning objectives and evolving threats despite resource constraints. Metrics establish accountabilities as programs that provide evidence of true deterrent value in the long term. Participation in peer networks facilitates comparing program maturity against frameworks. Collaboration transfers leading practices ahead of peers. Partnerships with research organizations import contextual threat intelligence. Consortia addresses mutual challenges, strengthening community defenses. Third-party quality assurance validations exercise programs identifying optimization opportunities. Outside expertise fills internal gaps, strengthening credibility. Standardization reassures leadership rigor aligns with objectives.

CHAPTER 20
Advanced Hands-On Exercises

Network Penetration Testing

Penetration testing, also known as ethical hacking, is a way for organizations to identify vulnerabilities in their external and internal systems from an attacker's perspective. Conducting network penetration tests allows security teams to find weaknesses before real attackers can exploit them. It will provide an in-depth overview of how to plan and execute network penetration tests in a legal and ethical manner.

PLANNING A PENETRATION TEST

Proper planning is essential for a successful penetration test. The most important step is obtaining written approval from leadership to conduct the penetration test. Clearly define the agreed-upon scope, timing, and goals of the test. Get sign-off on all activities to avoid any legal issues. Determine what systems and networks will be included in the test. Will it cover external internet-facing assets only or internal systems as well? Define an IP range or specific hosts that are in scope versus out of scope. Whenever possible, conduct penetration tests against non-production systems. Set up isolated testing environments that mimic the real infrastructure without risking operational stability. Virtual machines are ideal for this purpose. Inform all IT, security, and business teams who manage in-scope systems that a test will take place. Provide them with details on timing and expected testing activities.

ESTABLISHING TEST ENVIRONMENT

With planning complete, the next step is setting up your penetration testing environment. This should mimic your real infrastructure to the extent possible while remaining isolated. Deploy virtual machines (VMs) representing clients, servers, and network devices. Configure with the same OSs, services, and applications as production. Install networking tools like Nmap, Wireshark, and proxy servers on testing VMs; security tools like Metasploit, Hydra, and John the Ripper. Stand up isolated test Active Directory, DNS, and other directory services if applicable. Use for credential testing. Acquire target IP ranges, domains, and credentials specifically for testing use if it is safe to do so. Avoid production credential abuse. Configure a VPN or other secure remote access method for testers to connect to the environment. Isolate traffic. Try simulating a perimeter firewall, IPS, and network segmentation that is typical of client architecture. Document all IP ranges, credentials, and other sensitive test scoping details securely for future reference. With a functional isolated testing replica of real systems built, you are now ready to commence the next stage of active penetration testing.

FOOTPRINTING TARGETS

Active information gathering or footprinting is an important initial hacking stage. It involves passively and actively profiling your target networks to discover exposed vulnerabilities and identify high-value systems. Scan target IP ranges with Nmap to detect live hosts, open ports, services/banners, and OS details. Identify critical assets. Use DNS reconnaissance tools to find domain records, subdomains, internal hostnames, and employee emails. Run searches on public Pastebin/Github sites for leaked credentials matching your organization. Analyze network traffic with Wireshark filters to detect protocol and application metadata. Conducted web application scans with ZAP/Burp Suite to detect CMSs, versions, plugins, and configuration issues. Run search engine dorks and lookups on employee names combined with the company to find profiles/profiles mentioning technical details. Test for default/guessable credentials on IPMI, SSH, storage appliances, and other IOT devices.

VULNERABILITY ANALYSIS

With extensive information on in-scope systems, you can now begin active vulnerability verification. This includes tasks like Running vulnerability scanners authenticated/unauthenticated like Nessus, OpenVAS, and Nikto to detect known Issues. Test for common flaws using Burp Suite, ZAP, and other web app assessment tools. Look for SQLi, XSS, and brute force services/protocols with tools like Hydra to check default/weak credentials. Audit configuration of network devices, servers, and applications, checking for open shares/protocols. See if outdated/unpatched software can be exploited with Metasploit or other exploits. Enumerate API endpoints and payloads to detect flaws in authentication, access controls, and input validation. Run password cracking with John the Ripper on any captured hashes from services. Try to vertically escalate privileges by exploiting programming flaws and privilege issues.

ACTIVE ATTACKS

Once comprehensive footprinting and vulnerability scans are complete, shift testing to real active attacks. The goal is validating defensive controls by attempting to bypass them using hacking techniques an adversary may employ. Run phishing simulations with realistic mockups targeting different groups. Test delivery, click-through, and payload execution. Attempt SQL injection on web forms with encoded payloads exploiting stored XSS and sensitive data exposure. Run password spraying/cracking against accounts using common/dictionary passwords. Check for lockouts. Test social engineering via phone calls to IT/support pretending to be users with login issues requesting resets. Run password guessing against services, SSH keys, or remote access panels. Check account lockouts. See if external attackers could pivot inside once the beachhead is established by testing firewall rules to allow listing/delisting.

REPORTING AND REMEDIATION

Comprehensive documentation is critical throughout the penetration test but takes center stage during the reporting process. The final report should include an executive summary of key findings, identified risks, and recommendations. Details of testing methodology, scope, and assumptions. Include any scope changes that occurred. Heat maps or prioritized views of critical vulnerabilities detected. Break findings into critical, high, medium, and low severity. Documentation of each vulnerability discovered - name, description, impact, recommended remediation. Screenshots help illustrate issues. Data on any successful system access or privilege escalation achieved, including account credentials compromised. Observation on security control effectiveness - what controls worked, where gaps were observed. Append all technical output logs, scan results, and exploit code for traceability. Redact as needed. Provide a remediation timeline and contact for any compliance or legal questions related to findings.

Digital Forensics and Incident Analysis

With the rise of sophisticated cyber-attacks, having robust digital forensics capabilities is crucial for security teams. Should systems become compromised, organizations need to be able to properly investigate incidents while preserving evidence for potential legal actions. This process, known as digital forensics and incident response (DFIR), requires specialized skills and tools. We will outline best practices for conducting internal DFIR investigations along with methods for strengthening related competencies.

PLANNING AND PREPARATION

Being prepared well ahead of any incidents is foundational for DFIR's success. Some advance activities include defining response plans, training staff, and ensuring tools and resources are established. Response plans should document clear escalation protocols, roles, and responsibilities for colonization, eradication, and recovery phases. A dedicated incident response team keeps skills sharp through regular exercise scenarios, testing coordination, and technical skills. Tools like forensic workstations, write blockers, and licensed software get procured and tested. Retaining an external specialist team able to provide surge support if needed. Data sources requiring examination, like endpoints, servers, and network devices, get accounted for along with necessary access for responders.

INITIAL RESPONSE

The first priority upon detecting anomalous activity is containment to limit impacts. This involves isolating infected systems through firewall rules, blocking malware domains, and shutting down services. External law enforcement gets notified if necessary. Logs covering the scope of potential compromise get centrally collected and frozen to prevent modification. Accounting for time zone differences ensures evidence remains uncompromised. Full system backups replicate state for offline analysis containing live memory, disk images, and packet captures. The scope, preliminary assessment, and next steps are documented diligently from the onset. Attention now shifts to the detailed eradication and recovery phases.

ERADICATION AND RECOVERY

Once containment stabilizes the environment, root cause investigation commences. Using forensic tools, incidents are thoroughly analyzed to find patient zero indicators, lateral movement vectors, and exfiltrated data. Compromised or decoy systems replace tainted originals. Patches and configurations harden and deploy against similar re-infection. Network traffic patterns uncover suspicious patterns aiding remediation. Responders work closely with IT to execute streamlined recovery activities, restoring data and services once risks subside. Lessons learned throughout inform refining existing controls for prevention. Stakeholders throughout receive regular updates addressing concerns.

VALIDATION AND REPORTING

Before returning fully operational systems to end users, independent validation confirms environmental sanitization effectiveness. Tools replay hypothetical attacker steps confirming eradication success. Any restoration oversights get identified and addressed. A comprehensive incident report summarizes the timeline, root cause, impacts, and comprehensive remediation activities taken. Metrics track recovery speed and quality. Recommendations propose further risk reduction tactics. Legal counsel reviews content, ensuring compliance. Transparency to leadership and auditors maintains accountability and trust.

STRENGTHENING DFIR SKILLS

While planning prepositions teams for success, building hands-on skills sharpens competencies. Some recommendations include:

- Attend external training covering topics like memory analysis, malware reverse engineering, and legal/compliance practices. Pursue related certifications.

- Stand up an isolated lab environment to safely execute demo incidents using provided "malware" samples and disk images.

- Set up challenges like CTF events exposing responders to new tools and techniques through simulated compromises.

- Conduct internal workshops walking through example response plans, tool demonstrations, and skills assessments.

- Join industry groups and conferences to network with field experts and stay on top of the latest tactics and innovations.

- Publish sanitized case studies internally documenting real lessons applying book knowledge.
- Rotate response duties amongst qualifying staff, not retaining the same individuals forever, expanding comfort levels organization-wide.
- Maintain an incident response toolkit standardized Acronis, EnCase, Volatility, iptables, TCP dump, etc., for rapid deployment.

Consistent skill renewal keeps the function evergreen, addressing emerging risks. Maintaining proficiency gives confidence in handling sophisticated real-world attacks.

Red Team vs. Blue Team Exercises

Conducting simulated security exercises known as red-team and blue-team operations allows organizations to measure true defensive readiness. In realistic, structured scenarios, blue teams apply incident response skills, while red teams emulate adversary tactics. This promotes practical learning for both functions, improving overall security maturity.

PLANNING

Careful orchestration ensures safe educational experiences. Executive sponsorship establishes exercise goals aligned with strategic priorities such as third-party penetration testing, phishing resilience, or insider threat management. Realistic scope, teams, timeline, infrastructure requirements, and success criteria all require definition. Policies defining rules of engagement get jointly developed to avoid disruption. Discrete, isolated test environments mimic production environments however possible. Comprehensive pre-exercise intelligence gathering profiles targets. Resources such as virtual machines, network segmentation, and non-owned assets support exercise objectives.

BLUE TEAM PREPARATION

Blue teams strengthen incident response plans, tools, and coordination through internal workshops and external training. Response timelines, playbooks, checklists, and tool configurations get validated. Notifications standards integrate stakeholders. Response infrastructure includes dedicated workspaces, data stores, and tools for containment, eradication, and recovery. 24/7 staffing procedures address duty rotations. External exercises against provided scenarios test incident management lifecycles from identification to remediation. Internal awareness campaigns promoting indicators minimize real attacks. Analysts achieve response leadership roles.

RED TEAM OPERATIONS

Methodically stealthy, red teams mirror persistent adversary methodologies without disrupting operations. They profile targets, extract intelligence, authenticate, establish beachheads, move laterally, collect assets, and exfiltrate material realistically with patience. Techniques incorporate tools, exploits, social engineering, and creative hacking approaches. Infrastructure support intrusion kills focusing on specific policies, technologies, or user populations. Objectives concentrate on areas of greatest risk or control gaps. Teams receive legal and compliance guidance on permissible actions since these operations technically involve unauthorized access. Logs capture each step's outcomes and potential defenses requiring reinforcement.

EXERCISE SCENARIOS

Planned scenarios encompass routine and emerging threats faced. Examples may simulate external hackers, insider threats, physical access abuse scenarios, or supply chain attacks. Scenarios script general timelines yet encourage improvisation, enabling more unpredictable experiences that mirror the real world. Scenarios provide context, helping blue teams identify the activity as an exercise and respond appropriately versus treating it as a live incident. Prompts supply breadcrumbs for detection and response over multi-day timelines. Ultimately, blue team response outcomes measure strengths and weaknesses.

LESSONS LEARNED

Rich postmortems analyze successes and deficiencies throughout planning, execution, and response to identify specific recommendations. Logs capture red team operations and blue team analysis. Such postmortems objectively assess controls, coordination, policies, and competencies, noting validated strengths versus deficiencies requiring adjustment. Reporting codifies measurable takeaways across tactics, technologies, stakeholder involvement, and processes to present executives, lawyers, and auditors. Iterative exercise program refinement helps advance security maturity by addressing past inadequacies. Knowledge transfers equip all personnel to maximize readiness. Overall, these exercises prove impactful risk management and training activities.

EXPANDING SCOPING AND COMPLEXITY

To further advance skills and keep exercises fresh, organizations can progressively expand scope and complexity over time. Early events may solely focus on external or internal threats in isolation. Later iterations integrate blended scenarios combining social engineering, technical tactics, and physical security aspects. Expanding target profiles to cover additional infrastructure elements, geographical sites, business units, or critical partner ecosystems presents new challenges. Expanding red team membership with outside third-party assessors introduces unknown skill levels. More authentic experiences result. Lengthening exercise timelines from days to weeks mimics real adversary dwell times.

CONDUCTING POST-EXERCISE HOTWASHES AND TABLETOPS

To extract full value from events, facilitated Hotwashes and Tabletop discussions immediately after or in the coming weeks prove indispensable. Hotwashes promptly debrief key lessons while fresh.

Diverse participation from executive, security, compliance, and operational leadership fosters wide understanding and ownership of takeaways. Discussions focus on what went well, challenges encountered, and specific remediation plans. Tabletops weeks later evaluate remediation progress and address any lingering issues. Scenarios recap with an eye toward refining detected weaknesses. Stakeholder alignment validates priorities moving forward.

DOCUMENTATION AND REPORTING

Comprehensive records, including standardized logs, reports, meeting minutes, and exercise plans/documentation, establish institutional knowledge transference. Sharing sanitized case studies internally builds experienced communities of practice. Regular executive reporting tracks maturity metrics, exercise outcomes, remediation status, and upcoming plans. External reporting satisfies auditors and regulators. Dynamic programs evolve continuously with leadership support and oversight.

CONCLUSION

As we reach the end of our comprehensive five-part journey through the world of cybersecurity, I hope your mind is swimming with newfound knowledge - brimming with the latest tools, techniques, and insights needed to defend our digital landscape against increasingly sophisticated threats.

We covered vast ground together, from drilling cybersecurity fundamentals and policies to securing complex network architectures, cloud environments, and everything in between. You developed hands-on skills ranging from penetration testing to access management, gaining the experience needed to disarm threats in the wild. Importantly, you also cultivated senior leadership abilities to drive strategy and build robust security cultures.

Through each chapter, I synthesized over 15 years spent on the front lines securing critical infrastructure into actionable best practices, policies, and configurations. Backed by hundreds of detailed examples and case studies, this volume represents the most ambitious attempt to condense industry-wide learnings into definitive standard operating procedures.

Imagine the shift in your perspective. When you first started, there were gaps in connecting the cybersecurity dots. It wasn't clear how vulnerabilities spread across layers or how to foster organizational resilience. Now, you're seamlessly integrated across disciplines, armed with a multidimensional vision to proactively tackle risks. Thanks to leadership's precision in assembling cross-functional teams, secure cloud migrations, and effective business continuity plans, disruptions during incidents were mitigated. Compliance audits? They concluded favorably. Under your watch, the organization has become a shining example of cyber resilience in the industry.

As threats keep evolving ingeniously, so must our defenses evolve with sophistication. The concepts explored in this guide encapsulate timeless foundational principles. Confidentiality, integrity, and availability will always be the bedrock of information security. Risk management will continually guide resource allocation, and network segmentation will remain relevant. However, it's crucial to acknowledge that specific tools and techniques will become outdated without continuous learning.

I encourage you to build on these foundations through ongoing research. Evaluate each new headline against its strategic impact. Subscribe to threat intelligence feeds that monitor cybercriminal underground chatter. Attend conferences that capture cutting-edge zero-day exploit discoveries. Keep expanding your knowledge arsenal continually. The journey of cybersecurity is dynamic, and your commitment to staying informed ensures you remain at the forefront.

Moreover, let's enlist technology as our ally to make ongoing education more manageable. Automate routine tasks through scripting to free up valuable bandwidth. Transform modular tools into portable labs, saving time on reconfigurations. While implementing machine learning algorithms for pattern recognition can be challenging for humans, automation allows us to achieve scalability, providing more space for innovation.

Keep in mind that dynamism works both ways. While technology expands the possibilities of attacks, it also empowers defenders who cleverly utilize it. Stay eager to explore new techniques, from deception toolkits to adversarial machine learning, tipping the asymmetry back in your favor.

Just as information technology transforms industries, the implications of securing them also evolve. Uncharted frontiers like embedded systems in automotive, blockchain ledger technology, and quantum computing require pioneering security engineers like yourself to ensure smooth adoption. Bring lessons from the past, blend them innovatively with new challenges, and solve these open problems for the future.

I trust this guide has ignited your passion for this crucial domain. Channel that passion into structured knowledge, creating a protective impact that safeguards organizations from adversity. However, amid the turbulence, seek tranquility. Whether you discover the perfect vulnerability patch or catch a threat red-handed, celebrate these small wins whenever possible.

This concludes our time together. Go forth courageously at the frontier with skills to match your spirit. While cyber risks generate headlines, you now shape the positive headlines defending against them. From all of us working to preempt cyber threats, we thank you - and need more heroes like you in the arena protecting the assets we depend upon. This is your calling - seize it confidently and lead us forward one solution at a time!

APPENDICES

Glossary of Cybersecurity Terms

Antivirus Software: An application used to detect, prevent, and remove malware including viruses, worms, and trojans by scanning files and systems memory for known threats.

Application Security: The process of making apps more secure by finding, fixing, and enhancing the security capabilities of app source code through testing and configuration adjustments.

Attack Vector: The path or means by which an attacker can gain access to a computer or network server in order to deliver a payload or malicious outcome.

Backdoor: A secret method of bypassing normal authentication on a system, used to access a device or its data without the typical security checks.

Blockchain: A distributed ledger system recording peer-to-peer transactions in a verifiable, secure, and permanent manner across a network of systems with no central authority.

Blue Team: The group responsible for defending systems and networks against cybersecurity threats and attacks.

Bring Your Own Device (BYOD): The policy of permitting employees to use their personally-owned mobile devices like laptops and smartphones to access company resources and data.

Business Continuity Plan: Policies and procedures ensuring that critical business functions can continue during and after a disaster.

Chief Information Security Officer (CISO): An executive within an organization responsible for establishing and maintaining cyber and information security strategies and policies.

Ciphertext: Data or text that has been encrypted and is unreadable without decryption via a cipher algorithm using a secret key.

Cloud Security: Set of policies, controls, and procedures to ensure the security of data, infrastructure, applications, and services accessed through cloud computing environments.

Computer Forensics: The practice of collecting, analyzing, and preserving digital evidence found on computers, networks, and storage media in support of an investigation.

Confidentiality: The concept of ensuring sensitive data and files are protected from access by unauthorized users. Along with integrity and availability, it composes the CIA triad.

Cross-Site Scripting (XSS): An attack allowing malicious scripts to be injected into web applications and run within a victim's browser to access session cookies and other sensitive information.

Cryptography: The practice of techniques like encryption and hashing to secure digital information, transactions, and communications via transforming legible data into unintelligible ciphertext.

Data Encryption: The process of encoding data utilizing a cipher algorithm and secret key to transform it into encrypted ciphertext only retrievable by authorized parties.

Decryption: The process of decoding encrypted ciphertext back into usable plaintext that is readable and usable based on the cipher algorithm and secret key.

Denial of Service: An attack aiming to make systems or resources inaccessible to legitimate users by disrupting services.

Digital Certificate: An electronic document used to prove ownership of a public key for asymmetric encryption to securely transmit information over the internet.

Digital Forensics: The recovery and investigation of material found in digital devices to determine if the material contains any relevant evidence related to a cyber-attack or crime.

Distributed Denial of Service (DDoS): An attack using malware-infected computers to target and overwhelm systems with fake network traffic to exhaust bandwidth and crash services.

Domain Name System (DNS): An internet service translating domain names typed by users to machine-readable IP addresses that computers use to communicate with each other.

Encryption Key: A random string of bits created using an algorithm intended to keep sensitive data secure from unauthorized access. Decryption requires the right key.

Endpoint Security: Software solutions allowing organizations to monitor and secure remote user devices like laptops, desktops, and mobile devices.

File Transfer Protocol (FTP): A standard protocol used to transfer computer files between a client and server on a TCP and IP-based network, like over the internet.

Firewall: A network security system used to monitor data packets coming into and out of the network, filtering them based on a defined set of security rules.

Hacker: An unauthorized user who attempts to gain access to computer systems in order to steal, alter, or destroy data, often penetrating defenses using malware.

Hash Function: Produces a fixed length alphanumeric string (known as a hash value) based on variable length source data acting as a cryptographic fingerprint for verification.

Honeypot: Part of a network infrastructure configured as bait to lure cyber attackers and alert security professionals to malicious activity and techniques.

Insider Threat: The potential risk posed when a malicious insider with authorized access, like an employee or contractor, exploits internal resources.

Internet of Things (IoT): The network of internet-connected physical devices and sensors embedded in everyday objects enabling data collection and remote control.

Intrusion Detection System (IDS): Software that monitors networks and systems for suspicious activity and alerts administrators to potential threats in real-time.

Keylogger: Malware specialized to track keystrokes typed by users, capturing login information like usernames and passwords secretly.

Malware: Broad term for malicious software like trojans, viruses, spyware, and worms designed to infect devices and systems and cause damage.

Man-in-the-Middle: An attack where attackers insert themselves surreptitiously between communicating parties to siphon data by eavesdropping. Leverages lack of encryption.

Multi-Factor Authentication (MFA): Technique for confirming a user's identity that requires presenting two or more proofs like biometrics, tokens, or pin codes. More secure than using just a username and password.

Network Segmentation: Dividing larger networks into smaller subsections or subnets with defined trust boundaries to limit unauthorized lateral access between segments.

Network Sniffing: Passively intercepting network data transmissions traveling to and from devices on the same network segment allowing spying on traffic.

Penetration Testing: The practice of launching authorized simulated attacks on a computer system or network to uncover vulnerabilities before hackers exploit them. Also called pen testing.

Phishing Attack: Fraudulent messages disguised to appear as trustworthy correspondence to manipulate users into sharing login credentials or other sensitive data.

Plaintext: The actual readable message or data before being encrypted into coded ciphertext, also known as cleartext.

Private Key: The secret cryptographic key in asymmetric encryption is only known to the owner used to decrypt ciphertext or digitally sign messages.

Public Key: The cryptographic key distributed openly by the owner to anyone used to encrypt messages for the private key owner or to verify their digital signature.

Ransomware: Malicious software designed to deny system access to legitimate users by locking screens or encrypting data until a ransom is paid by the victim.

Red Team: The group that takes an offensive approach by emulating cyber-attacks against an organization to evaluate existing security measures.

Risk Assessment: The process of identifying, quantifying, and prioritizing information security risks faced based on severity and likelihood of occurrence.

Salted Hashing: Adding a random string of bits (called a salt) to an input before generating a cryptographic hash output to better protect against pre-computed hash attacks.

Security Operations Center (SOC): A facility comprising cybersecurity analysts tasked with 24/7 monitoring and defense of enterprise networks.

Session Cookie: A small piece of data sent from a website and stored on the user's computer temporarily to remember information between web pages. Often used to track login status.

Smishing: Receiving fraudulent text messages designed to trick users into revealing personal information or installing malware.

Social Engineering: Manipulative psychological tactics attackers use to deceive victims into sharing sensitive information or granting system access enabling cyber theft.

Software Defined Networking (SDN): An architecture decoupling network control functions from data forwarding functions allowing centrally managed dynamic reconfiguration.

Spear Phishing: Highly targeted variants of phishing attacks conducted against specific individuals based on reconnaissance and focused on gaining unauthorized access.

SQL Injection: An application security threat using malicious SQL code as input to access or manipulate restricted features of a database not normally accessible.

Symmetric Encryption: Cryptography uses the same secret cryptographic key to both encrypt and decrypt messages between parties unlike asymmetric schemes relying on private and public key pairs.

Trojan Horse: Malware is often masked as legitimate software that establishes remote access and control enabling cyber theft by gaining administrator privileges.

Two-Factor Authentication (2FA): A multi-factor authentication variant relying specifically on two different proof components like biometrics and tokens for more secure user access control.

Virus: Self-replicating malware attaching itself to clean files spreading exponentially between systems and devices by exploiting communication mediums.

Virtual Private Network (VPN): An encrypted network connection route established over a public infrastructure like the internet to enable secure remote access to private local area networks.

Vulnerability: Software, hardware, or procedural weaknesses in systems or applications that can be exploited by attackers to compromise security safeguards leading to breach or cyber theft.

Whitelisting: The practice of explicitly allowing some identified entities like users or applications while denying all others that are unsigned and unrecognized malicious entities.

Worm: Similar to viruses, these self-replicating malware programs spread automatically throughout networks without infecting files relying on security holes to propagate.

Zero Trust: A strategic cybersecurity approach centered around maintaining stringent access controls strictly validating every user, device, and network connection without assumptions.

Recommended Tools and Software

- Network Monitoring: Wireshark, SolarWinds, ManageEngine, Paessler PRTG
- Antivirus: Bitdefender, Kaspersky, Norton, McAfee
- Firewall: pfSense, UNTANGLE, SonicWall, WatchGuard
- Intrusion Detection/Prevention: Snort, Suricata, Darktrace, Vectra AI
- Endpoint Detection & Response: CrowdStrike Falcon, SentinelOne, Cynet 360
- Security Information & Event Management: Splunk, IBM QRadar, LogRhythm
- Identity and Access Management: Okta, PingIdentity, ForgeRock
- Data Loss Prevention: Digital Guardian, Forcepoint, Code42
- Security Operations Automation: Demisto, Swimlane, Siemplify
- Incident Response: Forescout CounterACT, FireEye Central MX
- Network Access Control: Cisco ISE, Forescout, Bradford Networks
- Security Awareness Training: KnowBe4, Cofense, Infosec IQ
- Password Management: LastPass, 1Password, Dashlane

Sample Security Policy Templates

Well-designed security policies translate strategies into enforceable standards protecting assets:

Acceptable Use Policy

This agreement outlines the responsible use of systems and internet resources aligned with privacy, ethical and legal standards. It restricts accessing inappropriate content like gambling sites, hate speech, or file sharing services illegally distributing copyrighted material. The policy authorizes monitoring of user activity and network traffic to ensure continual compliance. Violations may result in disciplinary action or legal penalties.

Data Classification Policy

This policy establishes a framework for classifying data into categories based on sensitive content to determine protective controls. Criteria for classification include confidentiality, criticality to operations, and impact of unauthorized disclosure or breach. Categories include confidential (highly sensitive internal data), private (personal user data), and public (non-sensitive information approved for public distribution). Data owners assign classification labels which are indicated visually through color coding, watermarks, or banners.

Access Control Policy

This policy institutes standards, scope, and responsibilities for granting, modifying, and revoking user access to systems and data based on necessity. It aligns access privileges with the principle of least privilege, granting only essential rights required for personnel to perform duties. Strict criteria govern elevated permissions like administrative access along with protocols for new user provisioning, periodic entitlement reviews, and revocation upon termination or transfer.

Incident Response Plan

This framework establishes procedures to detect, characterize, and respond to information security incidents like cyber-attacks, data breaches, or policy violations. It designates roles like an incident commander managing containment along with communications tasks like public relations and regulatory reporting. The plan outlines phases from initial preparation through post-incident analysis promoting orderly evidence-gathering supporting recovery.

Business Continuity Plan

This plan outlines procedures for restoring critical operations quickly following incidents disrupting normal infrastructure function. Extension of incident response plans activates teams tasked with minimizing downtime by restoring essential systems using alternate facilities, backups, or failover mechanisms. Regular testing verifies plan efficacy through simulated scenarios like widescale power outages or ransomware attacks.

Made in the USA
Las Vegas, NV
19 May 2024

90098666R00116